# OUT IN THE OPEN

# OUT IN THE OPEN

HENRY SCHAEFER

**OCEAN SPORT FISHING**
1620 Beaver Dam Road
Point Pleasant, New Jersey 08742

Printed in the United States of America

Ocean Sport Fishing
1620 Beaver Dam Road
Point Pleasant, NJ 08742

Editor .............. Henry Schaefer
Copy Editor............ Linda Barrett
Production....... Captain Matt Muzslay

# ACKNOWLEDGEMENTS

This book would not have been possible without the aid of Kenneth F. Lockwood, who published my first Out in the Open column in the old Newark Evening News; editor in chief Lloyd M. Felmly who didn't keep me chained to a desk; staff photographers Irving Tuttle and Horace Porter; and many other friends who shared my fishing and hunting adventures.

Illustrator Bill Canfield of the Newark Star Ledger sketched the cover picture. Leonard E. Rue III, who was gamekeeper for the Coventry Hunting Club above Blairstown when I first met him, supplied pictures as did Tuttle.

Also, the book would not have been possible without Lillian who never objected to my annual big game hunting trips, and shared in countless fishing adventures.

And last, credit also belongs to daughters Elizabeth and Lillian who used to sleep in the back seat on overnight trips to Maine in May, and Florida over Christmas vacation.

# FOREWORD

Henry Schaefer is different. It's true that Henry and I were both born in Newark. We both graduated from New York University. We both love to hunt and fish. We both worked for Outdoor Life. But that's where the similarity ends. I stayed at Outdoor Life and got caught in the New York rat race. But Henry didn't make a decision that would sometimes numb his senses. Instead Henry chose a path that would take him closer to the woods and waters and, ultimately, generate a dedicated following of readers who learned to love the Schaefer wisdom. I am one of them.

Henry was born in 1910. I arrived in 1934. That makes Henry 78 and me 54, which means I started reading Henry's Out In The Open when I was about 12. I remember vividly how Henry took me through the seasons every year. Henry told me about opening day of trout season. He told me about the streams, the number of trout being stocked, the hotspots and the bad spots. Henry gave me the same kind of information about small game season, duck gunning, deer season, striper fishing and anything else that was going on in the outdoors. I depended on Henry for the hard core reproting that helped me find good hunting and fishing in New Jersey for many years.

But, oddly enough, Henry's reporting is not what I remember best. Henry is still a topnotch reporter, but he's a better story teller and that's what I remember. I can easily recall those woodcock hunts, the fluke trips, the good days and the bad days on the trout streams. Henry always spun a good tale and in all those stories you could always find a good dose of the humility and wisdom that was and always will be the very best part of our Mr. Schaefer.

As the years passed and our careers crossed, I finally got to meet Henry and eventually hunt and fish with him. I want to tell you about a pheasant hunt a few years ago with Henry that will tell you more about this old hunter than I ever could with words. I arrived at the hunting lodge early and was sipping a cup of coffee while waiting for the other hunters to show up. My feet were starting to ache and I hadn't even started to hunt. I was wearing a brand-new pair of boots made of indestructible leather, nylon, Gore-Tex, rock hard lug soles and whatever else the manufacturer could conjure up. I never break in a pair of boots because there always seems to be some salesman selling me a new pair that will solve all my problems. My feet always seem to come out on the short end of these deals.

The door opens and in walks Henry and the first thing I notice is that his boots are about as old as he is. The boots are wrinkled leather, lace all the way from his instep up to just below the knee and they're covered with skunk grease or whatever to keep the rain out. Then I notice that Henry is

6

carrying a side-by-side with most the bluing worn off the barrels. I have a shiny new over-and-under with fancy screw-in chokes that they tell me are designed to kill more birds. My hunting jacket has enough noisy velcro on it to drive a deer herd right off the mountain. Henry sports a red-and-black plaid wool jacket that must have been a wedding present when he married Lillian. Are you beginning to get my message?

Henry has not been spoiled by time. He loves the woods and waters; he is comfortable there; he has aged gracefully with the outdoors without compromise. Henry's needs are simple because he has grown wise enough to realize that the most important thing in life is the experience . . . without the clutter of technology and sometimes interference of "progress." We should all be as lucky as Mr. Henry Schaefer.

In the following pages you will find the best of Henry's wit and wisdom. I know you will enjoy the adventures. The stores are from an age past and consider yourself fortunate to have discovered them.

It is also my hope that some of these tales will bring to memory some of your finest days afield . . . as they have done for me.

I wish you good hunting and fishing.

Vin T. Sparano
*Executive Editor, Outdoor Life*

# BIOGRAPHY
## *by*
## Howard Brant

HENRY SCHAEFER is a legend — an extraordinary gentleman who shall be remembered through the annals of time as one of our foremost sportswriters and learned outdoorsmen. An illustrious dean of the outdoor world.

We spent our formative years fervently reading Henry's "Out In The Open" column in the Newark Evening News and as a result of his written word we become indebted to him since Henry Schaefer was a major force in molding our very own outdoor personality.

Henry is indeed a jorunalist who prides himself in doing what he writes about. Unlike some sportswriters who merely sit at the copy desk and discuss the happenings of the outdoor world, such is not the case with Henry. He is habitually outdoors pursuing a variety of hunting and fishing opportunities available not only in the Garden State, but across the globe.

Henry was born in 1910 in Newark of German/Hungarian parentage and was introduced to the fishing world in 1915 by his grandmother who took him on sojourns to the Midland Beach Pier in Staten Island where he caught lafayettes with a hnadline.

As a teenager he trekked at every opportunity from Newark via trolley and shanksmare to Diamond Mill Pond in quest of trout and following his graduation from N.Y. University in 1933 with a Bachelor of Commercial Science Degree in Journalism, he began party boat fishing. Actually, his first offshore junket was aboard the Palace out of Hoboken.

During that era the late Kenneth Lockwood hosted the Out In The Open column for the Newark Evening News and he was most assuredly Henry's idol. Actually, it was Lockwood who was instrumental in turning his attention to the outdoor writing field.

But by then it was the Great Depression Years and jobs were scarce. Neverthe less, Henry still pondered the idea of someday writing about his first love — the outdoors. His opportunity finally came when, as a member of the Newark Bait and Fly Casting Club, he became its envy as a result of his trout fishing prowess with fly gear.

At that moment in time word reached the Newark Club that Lockwood was looking for a story about a kid who could catch trout with flies and

Henry told Lockwood he believed he could write such a story. Well, Henry did and received his first check from the Evening News for this piece of prose.

This very same story caught the eye of sports editor John Hall of the Elizabeth Daily Journal and shortly thereafter Henry landed a job with the Journal — he was on his way.

His writing career continued at Outdoor Life where he worked for a brief stint rewriting manuscripts. Then followed a 10 year period working on the Hudson Dispatch as a reporter and eventually Bergen County and city editor.

In 1946 Henry was appointed to the staff of the Newark Evening News and shortly thereafter, following the death of Kenneth Lockwood, Henry turned to writing the Out In The Open column — and the legend was born.

Henry Schaefer is a down-to-earth writer who writes about his very own personal experiences afield and the happenings of his fellow sportsmen. In addition, he possesses an uncanny memory and can recall incidents in time that normally appear only in encyclopedias.

Above all, his daily Out In The Open column remains vivid in the memory of so many sportsmen. His writings made us laugh, taught us important lesons, instructed us in outdoor ethics and sometimes even made us cry.

Henry was always a bird dog fancier and his many tales of his dogs were always enlightening. He was a trout fisher, too, as well as an avid deer hunter and saltwater angler.

We can well recall the story he wrote many years ago when he fought a giant trout for more than an hour at the Pequannock River. We can also remember his tale of how he tumbled from a tree stand and broke his wrist and the time he bagged a giant heavy-antlered buck in Livingston.

We can also recall the albacore he fought on fly tackle for several hours before it was successfully boated and his many ventures for whitetails in N.Y. State, Pennsylvania, Maine and N.J.

Henry's book, most appropriately titled Out In The Open, is the first he ever published and naturally it is well written and filled with ventures in the outdoor world. They are Henry Schaefer, sportsman, exemplary outdoorsman and authorative sportswriter. He writes from the heart with no frills and all his treatises are true. We can all learn something from the dean of outdoor writers.

Today in his twilight years, Henry continues to write for several local newspapers and national periodicals and his offerings continue to sparkle. He also remains an active member of the Outdoor Writers Association of America, the Metropolitan Rod and Gun Editors Association and the N.J. Outdoor Writers Association. And he still treks afield chasing upland game with his favored side-by-side double and further remains hard on the trail of trout and offshore gamefish.

We've had the honor and privilege of hunting and fishing with Henry in various corners of the world — from Winchester's Nilo Farms in Illinois to Remington Farms on Maryland's Eastern Shore — and we have personally witnessed his expertise with smoothbore, rifle and fishing gear.

However, through the years we never really praised him but we now like to take the opportunity to do so. Yes, Henry Schaeffer is a legend and we humbly thank him for providing us the opportunity to gain a better insight on the outdoor world as a result of his heartwarming personality, knowledge and writing. Thanks again, Henry . . .

Howard Brant
*Outdoor Editor, The Star Ledger*

# PREFACE

In an outdoors writing career spanning more than 50 years I've never been tempted to write fiction, because the things that really happen in the life of the angler and hunter are sometimes really stranger than fiction.

No matter how carefully I've planned my trips, they've often turned out not according to plan. Before I made my first moose hunting trip to Quebec my wife and I went out to buy an 18-cubic foot freezer. This was to a highly rated wilderness in which Jimmy Salvato had collected many bulls. As proof he had a half dozen mounted and for years they stared down at the customers in the old Paterson, N.J. Rod and Gun Store.

During 10 days of hunting and portaging from one beautiful lake to another I never glimpsed a four-legged creature of any kind, but at the end of the safari when I was walking along a trail back to our waiting truck I spotted a small deer in a country that wasn't supposed to have any.

Many how-to-hunt-deer books have been written by experts, but I've never really learned how to hunt them, at least not whitetails. Most of the deer that I have taken were driven to me by other people.

Many were running.

I lack the stalking skill of an Indian and I can't shoot a deer for everyone in the party as some of the big woods guides used to do but if I did see a buck I could often get it.

The soundest bit of advice I can give is practice shooting with the weapon you intend to use, whether rifle, shotgun or bow. You can't get too much practice.

Practice shooting with bow and arrow is easy and ditto for the shotgun. However, the telescopic sight has complicated things for the rifleman who used to practice with cast lead bullets and reduced charges of powder.

It used to be simple to crank up the micrometer peep sight for reduced charges, and bring it back down again for full loads. I was never able to accomplish this with a telescopic sight. After I had it zeroed in for full loads I found that the safest thing to do was to keep my fingers off the dials.

"Take a kid fishing," advises the American Fishing Tackle Manufacturers Association, but while this admonition has produced an army of new customers and will continue to do so, proceed with caution.

You may think that you know all there is to know about fishing, but don't be surprised if the kid you take out for his or her first trip catches the largest of the day, possibly the most, and with the wrong lure.

In the chapter The Farm Pond a young boy captures a northern pike on a small trout lure that his grandfather didn't think of using, and in Lillian's First Salmon a six-year-old confounds the experts by catching the only legal fish, on the surface and in the middle of a hot bright sunshiny day.

There really is somebody up there and HE takes care of kids.

## *Out in the Open*
## *With Henry Schaefer*

A compilation of fishing and hunting adventures spanning more than 50 years.

# CONTENTS

Lillian wasn't supposed to catch the salmon because she was trolling on the surface with a fly rod on a bright summer day when all of the fish were supposed to be in the depths.

# Lillian's First Salmon

"I want to go too, Daddy," said six-year-old daughter Lillian. This was in our neat white rental cottage on the shore of Rangeley Lake, Maine. Our little house was in a group of a dozen owned by Dwight and Ethel Sawin, formerly of Pennsylvania who had decided to spend their "golden years" as proprietors of a sporting camp.

They found their dream at the end of Greenvale Cove, only about a dozen miles from the village of Rangeley where there were a number of stores including the inevitable sporting goods and fly shop. What the Sawins bought, in addition to the six cottages and as many "Rangeley Lakes boats," a beach and a pier to which the boats were tied, was a comfortable house on the other side of the road, outbuildings and an ice house to store solidified blocks of Rangeley through an entire summer.

At that time Sawin appeared to be in his 60s and in excellent physical condition. Whatever his business had been in Pennsylvania, he was a former trap shooter. In Maine he was a deer hunter, and didn't buy any meat during the winter. From ice out to the end of the season he guided salmon and trout fishing parties.

While the Sawins might have found their dream layout through a real estate agency, I found it by falling out of a canoe.

On my first trip to Rangeley I stayed at a big camp and had my own guide and canoe, Bill Foster who did the paddling while I cast streamer flies. This was in May, shortly after ice out and the fish were right on the surface. Fishing was excellent and a four salmon limit rather easy to get.

One morning Bill and I found ourselves near the end of the cove and right over the bar that runs from shore to shore just beyond the Sawin's cottages. I foul hooked a salmon in a ventral fin and had a lot of difficulty leading it into Bill's net.

I leaned far over the side the better to do the stearing, and just as I saw the salmon slide into the net I slid out of the canoe, butt first. Rangeley was remarkably beautiful below the surface too, and I admired the bottom of the canoe and glad I hadn't turned it over. Then I saw my rod, reel and line come sinking down and I grabbed the rod and kicked my way up to the surface.

The first man I saw was Bill and the second was the inebriated gentleman who had been sleeping in another canoe while his guide paddled. He was wide awake now and was staring at me in disbelief.

"Well at least we got the salmon," I said. "No we don't," said Bill. "He fell out of the net while I was trying to get the boat balanced."

I picked up the rod from the bottom of the boat and started reeling in the line. The salmon was still hooked and came to the net without further acrobatics.

We decided to go ashore, start a fire, and dry my clothing, and that is how I discovered Sawin's dream layout. After I got my clothes back on and felt warm again I fell in love with the neat cottages in a sheltered cove of what was then an excellent landlocked salmon lake, where a good fly caster could easily take a dozen or more in a day.

There were also squaretails, brook trout averaging a pound with some up to three pounds or more. Before they were squeezed out by the introduced Sebago Lake salmon, Rangeley had been famous for huge squaretails.

Charles O. Hayford, who supervised construction of New Jersey's first fish hatchery at Hackettstown in 1912, still maintained a home at Oquossoc on Mooselookmeguntic Lake into the 1950s. He used to tell me stories of the huge squaretails that abounded in the Rangeley Lakes before the salmon took over.

One monster was fought all night while people holding torches looked on from other boats. It was undoubtedly a brook trout because the only other salmonid in the Rangeleys at that time was the now nearly extinct blueback, a much smaller species.

The huge fish broke loose before dawn, and nobody will ever know how big it was. It may have weighed 12 pounds or it may have been a smaller fish hooked in the tail.

According to old legends farmers used to net blueback trout by the wagon load before Maine introduced the brook trout which crowded out the bluebacks but the brookies grew much larger. They spawned in the feeder streams and grew to huge size in the lakes without competition from other species.

The wisdom of stocking competing species is debatable, but Maine stopped trying to improve the fishing after the salmon went in. It built a hatchery at Oquossoc where young Hayford learned to raise both brook trout and landlocked salmon. He was lured to New Jersey by anglers who went to Maine each season.

I loved the salmon and went to Maine every year with my wife Lillian and daughters Elizabeth and Lillian.

Before the children started going to school we went in May when the fish were still on the surface and where they could be caught by fly fishing.

But in 1950 both girls were in school and it was June when we got to Maine. I couldn't catch a fish on flies although Charlies Shaw of Boston, who rented a cottage next to ours was doing right well by trolling a wire line, a half dozen cowbells (spinners) and a big worm balled on a No. 6 Sproat hook.

One sunny morning I was getting ready to go trolling, and my wife was getting ready to go to town to shop with Elizabeth and Lillian, only the little one didn't want to go to town.

She decided she was going fishing too and told me so. She was tired of catching chubs and an occasional small trout from the dock, and wanted to go out on the lake to catch big fish.

I don't think there are many fathers who can say no to a six year old, but I knew she couldn't handle a wire line outfit. The only thing that the girl could be expected to handle was fly tackle, and the only lure that I thought might have a chance was a three-inch orange Flatfish. By trolling slowly, I thought the lure might work down as much as three feet.

Then there was another problem, good old Charlie, the deep trolling champion of our little community, who had been showing me up every day.

He saw my daughter down at the dock with her fly rod and brilliantly deduced that she was going fishing and hit upon a father-daughter tournament, his daughter and himself against Lillian and me.

I didn't think that this was such a hot idea since his daughter was old enough to handle a trolling outfit, and I was sure that Lillian's chances were marginal at best.

But anyway, we got the show on the road as people say, and we started trolling down our shore and up past Salmon Ledge. Nothing. Then we crossed the cove, diagonally, and rounded Haines Point. Still nothing.

We passed Doctor's Island and then headed down the main lake. My Davis Spinners were throbbing steadily and my nightwalker started being attacked by small salmon.

I caught a half dozen in a short while, the largest possibly a foot long, and all of them had to be tossed back. There didn't seem to be any legal fish that day.

But the little fish must have looked pretty good to Lillian, because in a plaintiff voice she asked, "Daddy, when am I going to catch a fish?"

I don't know what I answered, but what I thought was, "Little kid, you're not going to catch a fish."

Well, down the lake I turned the boat toward shore to head for Old Knothead, a dead tree that we used as a landmark. I was looking forward on the turn to search the shore, and then I heard her reel scream and the splash of a leaping salmon.

The fish was the first legal salmon of the day, and I was tempted to take the rod from Lillian, but only for a moment. It was her first salmon and she was either going to fight it out herself, or she was going to lose it.

Well, she handled that nine-foot rod to perfection, didn't try to stop the fish when it ripped line off the reel, and recovered line whenever she got the chance.

As you may have guessed, she got that tired fish up to the boat and daddy netted it.

Then we trolled back to camp, the first two people to quit for the day.

The others came in during the afternoon, and nobody else had either a salmon or a trout, not even good old Charlie and daughter.

I still have that orange Flatfish, mainly because nobody ever tried it after it caught Lillian's first salmon.

Inquisitive buck.

# *The Biggest Buck*

The first year I hunted from the Cabin of Dreams, situated half way between Greeley and Lackawaxen in the Pocono Mountains of Pike County, Pennsylvania, was 1939. That was the year I met Dominick Calleo of Lodi, N.J., later to become Capt. Dominick Calleo, a Highlands, N.J. charter boat fishing captain specializing on striped bass and bluefish.

In those days Dominick never worked during the New York, Pennsylvania, and the New Jersey deer seasons. He just hunted, every day, whether the weather was fit or not. He had bought a cabin on Kuhn Road, a dirt affair north of Greeley, which crossed a high ridge to the east and ran for four miles before it reached the macadam road along the Delaware River. The road ran through a wilderness well populated by deer and grouse.

The cabin was Calleo's home whether he hunted from its door, or drove to Sullivan County, N.Y. or Stokes State Forest in New Jersey. Also season long residents at the cabin were Dominick's brothers Louis, John and Pat. Invariably there were four or five guests, and from 1939 and about 25 seasons thereafter, one of them was I.

To say we hunted hard would be an understatement. To say we were all successful would also be an understatement. Deer in Pennsylvania in those days were extremely plentiful, in fact they were too plentiful, and the state game commission was generous with seasons for antlerless deer in addition to the two week bucks only season.

The state experimented with limited antlerless seasons but in 1940 all deer except spike bucks were legal for the entire two week season.

The game commission wanted to cut that huge deer herd drastically to bring it safely back within the winter carrying capacity of the range, and without doubt more deer were killed in Pennsylvania than in any season before or since. The limit was one deer per license and it seemed that everybody who owned a license in 1940 filled it, even the grandmothers and school girls who bought licenses for that season.

In our own "neck of the woods" after three days it was impossible to travel in any direction for more than a few hundred yards without finding discarded deer entrails. As I remember there were 15 hunters at the Cabin of Dreams and every one went home with a deer.

We all believed that the state had been too generous and that the hunting would be poor the following year. It was on the slow side in 1941, but the herd came back fast after that.

Permits for the special antlerless seasons that followed were ample, and since they were available to all license buyers regardless of what state they lived in, we all got doe permits every year on the day they went on sale.

We all hunted hard and the four brothers and I managed to fill licenses every year. However, bucks with big racks were a rarity in our area, and I can't remember more than a half dozen that really had trophy heads.

Dominick was the hardest hunter, first out of the sack each morning and the last to get back to the cabin at night. He was a still hunter who roamed both sides of the mountain and worked the ridges and the heavy cover in the woodland swamps where bucks take refuge during the day.

Brother John on the other hand seldom got out of the cabin before 9 a.m., and then he didn't travel far. He preferred to post in cover on a nearby ridge and wait. However, he got a few very good racks all within easy dragging distance of the cabin. It puzzled us then, but over the years there always were a few bucks hanging out in heavy cover near the cabin, and in a dense swamp just behind the village of Greeley.

Brother Louis was no great traveler either, but on post he could sit for hours without moving any part of his body. Most people who sit betray their presence by moving their hands or twisting their heads, but not Louis. Once two does moved close and then dropped to the ground to take a nap.

When I got back to camp that afternoon I admired the fine buck that Louis had hanging in the apple tree and he told me the story. "I figured that that was where the deer went to sleep so I lay down on the ground too," Louis said. "When I woke I saw this buck lying a short distance away so I shot him. It was hard to do with the rifle in one hand, and the other braced against the ground."

I shot little bucks in 1939 and 1940, and little did I think that 20 years later, still hunting from the Cabin of dreams, I would shoot a fine trophy buck.

**Heading for timber.**

The story starts with another buck, strangely, a tame one. There always seemed to be a few tame deer near the cabin because only about a mile away was the Pine Tree Cottage, an inn with tennis courts and always a lot of summer vacationers. Most of the time these tame deer were does and fawns but in December of 1959 there was a buck.

When I got to camp on the Sunday before deer season the first thing everybody told me was the story about the tame buck that had been around the cabin all fall. Tony Squeo of Highlands, one of Dominick's pals, reported that he had seen the buck in the yard when he went out to throw away potato peelings.

I sat down to eat and presently two of the younger fellows came through the room with rifles, announcing that they were going outside to sight them in. They were hardly outside before the war started. Both of them were shooting as fast as they could and since they were so close it sounded plenty loud.

The rest of us leaped from our chairs and ran to the bedrooms to look out of the back windows. There is an open field with a couple of apple trees, stretching about 60 yards to the remains of a stone wall behind the cabin. Beyond that is a tiny brook and beyond the brook the forest climbs quite steeply for a half mile.

We saw the buck running up through the woods, none the worse from his experience. The guns of the two sports were now silent. They were out of ammunition.

That wasn't the end of it. Later the buck came back again and one of the men took a shot at it from a bedroom window, announcing that he thought he had hit it.

I didn't sleep too well that night and I doubt anybody else did either. They were all thinking about that buck. Everybody wanted him, and at least three men had already tried to kill him.

The hunting had changed over the years and not for the better. Deer were much scarcer. Where there had been just one other camp and a farm on the far end of the road, there were now a half dozen other camps, all full of hunters.

Just a few years before a natural gas pipeline had been laid right through our beloved hunting country. To accommodate the pipeline a swath as wide as a highway had been cut over our mountain and through the woods. The pipeline runs east and west about three quarters of a mile north of the cabin.

**In full flight.**

Whereas, in the old days, we had seldom seen another hunter back there, it is now over-run during deer season. Hunters park along the highway and use the pipeline as a road to lead them up the mountain.

Most of them post within sight of the pipeline. They don't kill many deer, but their presence has drastically changed hunting in that area.

Everybody in camp set out for that tame buck at the legal shooting time of 7 a.m. on opening day. I took a stand on the side of the mountain three quarters of a mile above camp. It was very cold but there was no snow. Two hours went by during which I neither saw nor heard anything.

Suddenly there was a volley of shots, the sound coming directly from camp. I was sure that someone in camp had killed the buck. But a few minutes later there was another volley, this time much closer.

After a few minutes there was a third volley. This time the rifles were barking so close to me I thought I should have been able to see the hunters. I couldn't see them but I soon heard them talking. There seemed to be only two and from what I could hear it seemed that they had killed the deer.

I left my stand to take another farther away, but by noon curiosity got the better of me and I went back to camp. As anticipated, the carcass of the tame buck, a small five pointer, was hanging in the apple tree by the front door.

Dominick, Tony and Henry Mewes of Atlantic Highlands were in camp. Mewes was ill in bed. Dominick and Tony were in the living room. Both were happy, particularly Dominick who had killed the buck.

I sat down to a dinner of ham and potatoes while they unfolded one of the craziest deer stories I have ever heard.

They had hunted for nearly two hours, had seen nothing and decided to go back to camp. Dominick wanted to use the outhouse which was to the left and slightly in front of the camp. Parked haphazardly in the front yard were the half dozen cars of the hunters.

Tony was in the living room, doing nothing of much consequence, when he happened to look out of the front window. There was the buck, eating grass between the automobiles

You or I might have eased the front door open and shot the buck, but Tony didn't do that. He opened the door and shouted, "Hey Dom, the buck is in the front yard."

Dominick, who had his rifle with him, kicked open the outhouse door but the buck, between the cars and with head down, still eating, was not visible

"Where is he?" Dominick demanded.

"He's right there," shouted Tony, and at that moment decided to get his own rifle, which he did and walked out on the porch.

The deer lifted his head and stared at Tony. Dominick waited for the buck to walk clear of the car and was just about to squeeze off a shot when Tony fired at a range of 25 feet, missing the deer completely. Both men emptied their guns, frightening the deer which ran into the woods.

That accounted for the first volley I had heard. Twice more they fired when they saw the deer in the woods and finally Dominick dropped it.

It had been a crazy day but it wasn't over.

I got up from the table at 12:30, took my Winchester Model 70 .30/06 and walked out behind the camp. I crossed the little field, went through a hole in the stone fence, and paused to look at the little stream.

Suddenly I heard something coming. It had to be a running deer and it was making quite a noise in the frozen leaves. The deer came into view and mostly what I saw were antlers, a big rack.

The buck was running furiously along the top of a ridge about 40 yards away and I missed him with the first bullet. I slammed in another cartridge and this time the bullet smashed his spine. He rolled down the ridge toward me and came to rest in a little hollow in the ground.

He was dead.

I looked at the buck and then turned to look at the cabin less than 100 yards away. I thought of the long years of hunting when I had combed miles and miles of woods from dawn till dark without seeing one as good as this one in our own back yard.

He had a perfect eight-point head but twice as big as the normal good eight pointer. At the end of the week, when Dominick went into town, he learned that a number of Greeley hunters had been looking for the big buck because he was commonly seen all fall in the fields behind the town.

Like the little five pointer, he didn't seem to be afraid of people.

**The biggest buck.**

The author with a tiger trout taken in Lake Solitude below the Ken Lockwood Gorge.

# The Biggest Trout

It happened on what was then a wild and unfettered portion of the Pequannock River as it flowed through the Newark Watershed close to the superintendent's quarters at Charlottesburg, which doesn't appear on a map. Not much of the watershed, a wilderness, is named on maps because few people live there.

The watershed portion of the stream at that time was stocked once a year with brown trout from the Charles O. Hayford State Fish Hatchery at Hackettstown, but nobody could fish without the consent of the superintendent.

Consequently it got next to no publicity from the late Kenneth F. Lockwood, the first Out in the Open editor of the defunct Newark Evening News, who died in 1948. As the second and last editor of the column I carried on the tradition because of the extremely limited public access.

The gravel, rock and boulder filled stretch produced enormous hatches of flies, and the few who fished it rated it the best dry fly water in New Jersey. It flowed into the last impoundment on the watershed and the water that wasn't piped to the cities continued as the Pequannock River, still stocked wtih trout from Route 23, Smoke Rise to Butler.

Lockwood's memorial is on the stretch of the South Branch of the

Raritan, Califon-High Bridge, which is named after him, and which was his favorite stream in New Jersey.

Like most people in those days he was a weekend fisherman, and he spent most of his weekends fly fishing for trout in the Catskills.

I seldom fished the watershed stream but one spring day three of us elected to go there because we were sure it wouldn't be muddy, and equally sure that most of the western streams, after days of rain, would be. With me were Alexander (Axle) Gromack, now of New City, N.Y., and Donald Schulte, now of North Myrtle Beach, South Carolina.

We were all fly fishing, not because we were purists, but because the trout that lived there didn't seem to know that worms and salmon eggs were good to eat.

On this day, in the high water, they weren't all that crazy about fake insects either, and after a couple of hours of casting none of us had had a touch. So we held a council and decided to move on to the Musconetcong River, which we thought would be the clearest of the western streams.

My two buddies had been fishing a big and deep pool and as they vacated it I told them I wanted to make a few casts, just to see if one of my two wet flies would work. My tail fly was a Black Gnat size 14, and the dropper a Pale Evening Dun 12.

The pool was made to order for a right-handed caster, water rushing in from the rocky run on the right and sweeping in a left curve over the deep water, and then shoaling at the tail before entering rapids.

Fifty yards below was a small island with the main flow, as usually seems to be true, raging on the far side. I made a mental note of that in anticipation of what would probably happen if I should hook a big fish.

I didn't have long to wait.

On the very first cast, as my deep drifting flies passed over the big boulder I knew was in the pool, I felt a heavy weight. It felt like a snag but then the weight moved deliberately up stream, turned to move down to the tail, and turned to come back to the original spot where it settled to the bottom and stopped.

In frigid water up to my waist I was hooked into something heavy resting on the bottom. I knew that it was fish, possibly a huge trout, or maybe something else. For the next hour I tried to get that thing to fight, but all it wanted to do was lie on the bottom with an occasional journey to visit both ends of the pool, and then wind up on the bottom for another long rest.

I wasn't happy about the situation at all. It was obvious that the fish could leave the pool whenever it wished, and if it elected to move down through the rapids there was no way I could stop it short of that damn island.

32

And even if it ran down my side of the island, there wasn't another piece of quiet water, or an eddy, for a half mile down.

But I wanted to get a look at the fish, at least. So I backed slowly toward shore, and wonder of wonders started moving the fish shoreward, too. I got it into about four feet of water and peered down along the leader to see something small flashing.

It was a chub swimming in furious circles around the leader, with the dropper fly hooked in its mouth. Whatever was at the far end of my double hook-up was invisible.

And then the biggest trout I ever hooked in a New Jersey stream decided to go back to the middle of the pool and rest his belly on the bottom again. As he moved off he flashed his side, double the width of the palm of my hand, with black spots that looked as big as the nails on my fingers.

It was a brown trout.

A long time later Don appeared to find me sitting at the edge of the pool, legs in the water, with rod bent double against an inanimate object holding the bottom slightly downstream.

"How long have you guys been gone?"

"Oh, about an hour."

"Well, Ive had a trout on ever since you left."

Then Axle appeared and as soon as he got the message grabbed his landing net and advanced to the edge of the water. I implored him not to try to get a far too small net under a fish that was as green as it was when first hooked.

At that time the trout was lying about a dozen feet from shore in about two feet of water. It was just beyond a rock that was two feet wide. Axle had gone down on hands and knees to crawl to the edge of the bank and look.

"Do you see the trout?" I asked.

"Yes," said Axle. "I see him. His head is above the rock and his tail is below the rock." At the very least that big-jawed wide-bodied male was 28 inches long. At the very least it weighed seven pounds.

I told Don that if I had any chance to get that fish it must be forced to fight the current. I begged him to throw rocks at its tail to get him into the current, but Don was reluctant. "If he turns and runs down the rapids then it will be my fault," he said.

The twirling chub had disappeared from the dropper fly, and after a little while the tail fly lost it hold and line and empty leader came flying back into the air.

It started to rain as we walked in silence back to the car, and thence on to the Musconetcong. I can't remember what, if anything we caught there.

One last look.

# How Big Do They Come?

Finn H. Magnus, a native of Denmark who immigrated to America to beome a factory worker to wind up as an industrialist and the country's "harmonica king," had never seen a wild animal larger than a cottontail when he first went to Newfoundland on a hunting trip with me in 1953. He had become a big game fisherman of considerable importance. He owned a fine boat and competed successfully in East Coast big game fishing tournaments.

However, firearms and hunting were untried adventures. I was sure that he would like big game hunting and helped him outfit at Abercrombie and Fitch in New York Ctiy for his first trip. In late September, as was my wont in those days, we flew from New York to Gander, Newfoundland, where we met our outfitter Edgar Baird, and the following day flew to our camp on the shores of Newton Lake, which was at that time in the heart of excellent caribou country where moose were also to be found.

That very afternoon Finn shot and killed his first big game animal, which he called a "cariboose," actually a stag caribou. It had a nondescript head but the new hunter was proud.

Possessor of a double license, which cost all of $75 in those days, Finn then set about the task of finding a bull moose. It proved to be more elusive than the caribou.

Several days later he was hunting in mixed woods and tundra barren country west of the lake with three guides, Matty, Paul and Bill Joe. The reason he had three guides was because there was a surplus of help, Finn and I were the only hunters in camp.

At mid morning, having seen nothing, the four were resting in an open area surrounded by a dense forest of spruce and fir. Suddenly there started a terrific din in the forest, much bellowing and grunting, and the investigating guides determined that the cause was a bull moose and a cow with calf.

A plan was rapidly devised to have Paul and Bill Joe drive the bull out of the woods and toward Finn, who was to stay in the open with Matty.

So two of the guides circled the area where the moose were carrying on and Finn waited. In due course, as Finn told the tale, "a tremendous black animal" came lumbering out of the woods and straight toward him. He raised his .30/06 scope sighted Model 70 Winchester but Matty, with a loud whisper, hissed, "don't shoot, That's the calf."

Finn watched it run off.

Within moments, Finn said, "another and much bigger animal came running out." Again he raised his rifle but again Matty cautioned, "don't shoot, That's the cow."

"How big do they come?" asked Finn. The cow had looked as big as an elephant. When the bull, shortly after, came rolling out along the same course the other two moose had taken, he saw for the first time how big moose really do grow.

"Shoot, shoot" ordered Matty, and Finn obliged, hitting the bull fairly in the chest and down it went. Within less than a week after leaving his home in Essex Fells, N.J. the novice sportsman who never before had seen big game of any kind had succeeded in bagging a stag caribou and a bull moose.

Neither had a head that would make any record book but Finn didn't really care. He was fairly launched on his new career of big game hunter.

Rack of the moose that charged.

Going for a swim.

# The Moose That Charged

According to most gun writers moose are not dangerous and while a bull might walk around stiffly and look menacing he is really harmless as a kitten. They explain that the reason a bull doesn't seem to be afraid of people is because he can't see well, but in many trips to Canada and the American Rockies I learned that moose can see very well and they can be dangerous, both sexes, but especially bulls in rut.

However reassured by the literary experts, I wasn't the least bit afraid of moose when I first started hunting for them in northern Quebec, and I couldn't understand why the French Canadians and the Indians seemed to hold them in respect.

I never had any reason to be afraid of moose in mainland Canada because during two long trips I didn't see any. I didn't start seeing any in Newfoundland either on my first tirp, but on my second, in 1951, I started seeing a few moose but a lot of caribou.

Moose were scarce in the interior of the hugh island at that time, but the guides came from settlements on the south shore where there were a lot of moose. They talked about the big animals in awe, and I couldn't understand why.

I started scoring with caribou and moose in succeeding seasons all without incident, and once I became very angry at my guide who refused to go into heavy timer where a rutting bull was bellowing. Stanley was badly frightened and motioned that we circle the bull into a clearing, but the bull never came out of the woods and since I could no longer hear him I didn't go into the timber to look.

While I started rifle hunting for deer with a Savage .303 lever action rifle I went over to a Winchester Model 54 in .30/06 caliber after I started handloading, and had complete confidence in 180 grain bullets for all game up to moose and elk. However, a bullet fired at a large male black bear blew up in the shoulder, but I managed to kill the animal with a brain shot as he was running away on three legs.

Perhaps a 200 grain bullet would have broken both shoulders but I stuck to 180 grain bullets pushed by 57 grains of 4350 Du Pont powder, first in a Model 54 Winchester. It had a Lyman 48 peep scope which I used without an aperture. At three degrees of elevation the rifle was zeroed in for 200 yards with either factory loads or hand loads. Elevated to 19 degrees the rifle was zeroed in for 150 grain lead alloy bullets pushed by 12 grains of Hercules Unique powder.

I fired thousands of handloads each summer and had full confidence both in my equipment and ability to use it.

But iron sights had gone out of style and for the 1957 season I bought a Winchester Model 70 and equipped it with a four power Bausch & Lomb telescope. I practiced with this rifle but continued to use the peep sight equipped rifle for reduced loads.

In the fall I went back to Newton Lake in Newfoundland and on the very first afternoon I shot a fine caribou with 29 points and a double shovel. He came trotting by at about 75 yards, and after we dressed him out and got him off the ground to cool I got two ptarmigan with head shots, and passed up a bull moose with small antlers.

Outfitter Edgar Baird who lived in Gander had a fine camp on an island on Newton Lake and after an early breakfast the next morning guide Mike Joe and I got back into our canoe for the trip back to the caribou. Mike and his brother Bill had become good friends of mine after several hunting seasons. They were both in their thirties, hard working and proficient.

We paddled up the lake for a couple of miles to the inlet stream and then ascended the stream for a few hundred yards where we beached the canoe, and started walking up a well traveled game trail that led through heavy forest and up a sharp incline to reach the muskeg that covers most of interior Newfoundland.

We had covered the caribou carcass with spruce boughs to hide it from the eyes of ravens and bald eagles and found it untouched. The evening before I had seen the antlers of a moose flashing in the light of the setting sun and we headed in that direction.

Beyond where the moose had been the land dropped sharply into a deep valley which we called the Valley of the Giants because we saw moose there on every visit.

It is a big valley, several miles across and the floor is covered with grass. There are stands of stunted spruce and fir but no high trees.

When we reached the edge of the valley we saw three moose below us. They were a bull with a pretty good head, a cow and a calf, all grazing and

40

moving to our left.

Mike didn't think that we'd be able to intercept the moose, but I wanted to try and we ran and hopped down the hill at breakneck speed. When we got to the valley bottom the animals were nowhere in sight.

I started looking for them and when I turned one little patch of trees I saw the bull standing on what appeared to be open ground 300 yards away. He was facing me three quarters on, and looking at me.

The shot had to be taken off hand, but I wrapped the sling around my left arm as tightly as possible and held for the left shoulder. At the shot the moose dropped out of the glass and when I put the rifle down I saw nothing but clumps of trees and grass.

"There never was a deader moose than that one." said Mike as we started walking to the spot. Half way there the cow and the calf jumped up from their beds and started trotting away. I went for my camera in my packsack, but before I could reach it the moose were too far for pictures.

That interruption got us slightly off course and when we got to the spot where we thought the moose had fallen we found nothing. I kept looking into spruce and fir clumps and walking around in the open trying to find a 1,00 pound animal that had be come invisible.

Then I got what I thought was a bright idea. I told Mike I was going back to the spot where I had taken the shot, look at the spot where the moose had been standing, and then walk right to it.

I thought Mike was following me. He wasn't. I had gotten almost back to the spot from where I had fired the shot when I heard Mike call. I turned and was startled to see that he was still in the place where I had seen him last. He was pointing into a thicket.

So, Mike had found the moose and I started marching back, looking mostly at my feet as they carried me over the damp and dangerous muskeg. The next time I looked up I saw a sight I still see in nightmares.

Mike Joe was coming in my direction, running as he had never run before and probably never did again. Fifty fet behind Mike came the bull, traveling at even greater speed. His antlers were low to th ground like the cowcatcher on an old steam locomotive.

The bull was coming every fast, running as if there were nothing wrong with him, and I couldn't shoot because Mike was in the way. Headlines flashed through my mind: MOOSE KILLS MAN STUPID YANKEE TO BLAME.

Then the first of three miracles happened. The left shoulder collapsed and the moose went down on his fore end. The hind quarters remained standing, and Mike was able to reopen the gap between him and his pursuer.

But the moose didn't stay down. he regained his front legs and came on strong again, rapidly closing the distance between him and his target. Then the second miracle happened. The moose went down again, hind legs standing as before.

Again Mike gained ground, and again the bull regained all four legs and came on again. At this point Mike passed me about 40 yards out. It couldn't possibly have been so, but it seemed to me that his pack sack straps were horizontal, and that the sack was straight out from his back.

At this point I had a clear shot and the target was exactly the same, the left front shoulder. The moose had halted when he saw me and I drove another bullet into that shoulder.

Instead of falling the moose lowered his antlers again and now he was coming right to me, fast. In desperation I fired two bullets into the right shoulder, and saw it tremble like a big gob of black gelatin but the bull didn't go down.

Then I tried for a dead on frontal brain shot and the third miracle happened. I hit the small target right on the nose and the bull dropped dead.

He fell 25 feet away with five bullets in him. There was only one round left and that was in the chamber. Mike came back and the two of us started the big job of dressing out the moose and skinning it before quartering.

We hung the quarters in trees and covered them with boughs of spruce and fir so birds wouldn't be able to see them. This was the second day of a six day trip and we were busy for three days there after carrying moose and caribou quarters back to our canoe.

Bill Joe helped but it was still hard work.

There were other sticky incidents and always with moose and never with grizzly bears, which I believe are far more plentiful in the Bob Marshall Wilderness in Montana than the U.S. Fish and Wildlife Service seems to think.

Another charge was actually a determined walk by a bull that had spotted three of us sitting at the edge of woods. Perhaps 400 yards away he saw us and started approaching. His tongue was wagging and his eyes glowed like the eyes of a dying deer.

I asked the 18-year old boy in the group who had an unfilled license if he was going to kill the bull. He said he didn't want it. The guide had no gun. I didn't want to kill the bull either but felt we were in bad trouble if nobody did.

So I shot the bull and when we skinned it we found that it was full of gangrene from many wounds in the body suffered in a losing fight with another bull. The moose was dying on his feet and I am sure he had intended to kill us.

The hide was full of holes and we placed it over the body and left him there.

# The Worthless Fly

Don Schulte of North Myrtle Beach, South Carolina, at various times during his working years was a merchant and real estate salesman, but at all times he moonlighted as a fly tier, specializing in dries, and built up a respectable business among north Jersey purists while he was still living in Livingston.

His house was close to mine and for years we fished the famous streams in the hilly northwestern counties, the Musconetcong, South Branch of the Raritan, Rockaway, Big Flat Brook, Paulinskill and Pequest. Also we fished in New York State with yearly April pilgrimages to Cold Brook, Hammondsport, and Catharine's Creek, Watkins Glen, for the spring run of rainbow trout.

I had a lot of faith in Schulte dry flies, wet flies and nymphs, but he never seemed to get the hang of streamer fly construction, or so I thought, so I tied my own. I fancied myself quite an expert, but must admit streamers and bucktails are simple compared to, for instance, No. 18 midges.

I didn't like my friend's streamers, but when he started making feather fish I thought he had really stripped his mental gears. The fake fish were reallly tied well, three feathers flat along a longshank hook, a bit of hackle at the head, white enamel eyes, and a tail achieved by tying a knot beyond the bend of the hook and trimming with a tiny scissors.

He presented me with one of his masterpieces, but it looked like an artificial fish to me and I was sure no trout would be fooled by it. The pulsating feathers or hairs of streamer flies work because they give the illusion of life.

I was sure Don's stiff feather replica of a minnow was worthless, and so I placed it in my box of streamers and promptly forgot about it, for a few seasons.

And then came a glorious spring morning on Big Flat Brook when brown trout were in a feeding frenzy and taking streamers. During the course of a few hours I managed to lose several flies and then found to my dismay that the only thing left in the box was Schulte's feather fish.

I decided to use it, and after losing it, I would start nymph fishing and take and release a few more trout.

A short distance below the Route 206 bridge there is a large, deep pool, with the foundation of an old building on the side. At one time there probably was a mill there. I was on the far bank, casting toward the road. There were several anglers above and below the foundation, but no one else on my side.

After several casts there came a solid strike and then just heavy weight, with none of the gyrations of the brown trout that I had been catching. This was a heavy fish and after it decided to move it was upstream. This would have pleased me except that there was a stick jutting above the surface above the fish.

The course that she was taking was several feet beyond the stick, and I was sure that Schulte's not so worthless fly was about to be broken off. But wonder of wonders, when the line reached the stick it bent to permit the line to clear.

The fish was still on. It remained deep throughout the long struggle but after what seemed like 15 minutes it started to tire and I saw that it was a big rainbow, a trophy by New Jersey stream standards.

The landing nets New Jersey stream anglers carry are designed for fish that seldom are larger than a pound, 14 inches, but this four-and-a-half pound two-foot hen could not be guided into the net for another 10 minutes.

She was just the right size for a wall mount, and is still on display, but without the Worthless Fly.

Somehow, I lost it.

The author and Capt. Otto Reut with a little tunny taken on a light bamboo fly rod.

Betty Schaefer boats a bluefish for her sister Lillian (left), caught by trolling with Capt. Charles Eble of Barnegat Light.

Spotted through binoculars in fading light this Wall Pond, Newfoundland, black bear was first mistaken for a moose.

Hastily re-rigged fluke tackle was used to take these tuna from a big school surface feeding off a jetty at Avon.

**This bluefin tuna was caught on a tinker mackerel aboard Capt. Jack Early's party boat Early Bird out of Highlands.**

Guide Don Spears of Dubois, Wyoming, and the author with "My First Bull Elk" taken just below treeline in the Shoshone National Forest.

# My First Bull Elk

Back in 1956, Dubois, Wyoming, looked exactly like a cattle town in a Grade B western movie. However, instead of only one saloon it had six and on Saturday night they were all filled with cowboys, cowgirls and Indians from the Shoshone reservation not far from town. There was only one jail and on Saturday night that was filled too.

Patrons had the option of dancing to western music played by live musicians, playing poker with silver dollar chips, or just talking and drinking at the bar. The favorite topics of conversation were cattle, women, hunting and fishing. There were mounted heads of elk, mule deer, moose and antelope in every saloon, as well as trophy size trout.

On the Wind Rinver on one of the main roads leading to Yellowstone National Park, Dubois is on the threshold of the Shoshone National Forest where the scenery is spectacular and the hunting just about as good.

Mule deer and elk abound. Moose are plentiful. Bighorn sheep are numerous enough to make ram hunting an almost sure bet, provided a hunter is lucky enough to draw a permit. During the 1950s there were only limited numbers of permits available by lot for elk, moose and sheep in the Wind River region. The sheep permits were hardest to come by.

It was my first trip to the Rocky Mountains and I was having the time of my life even though, during my first week of hunting, I had failed to get a bull elk. I outfitted with Bob Tripp, a transplanted New Jerseyite, who operated a dude ranch and motel on the outskirts of Dubois. Bob had picked me up at the airport at Cheyenne, and on the drive back to his ranch through miles of flat prairie I started seeing antelope, a lot of them.

In addition to my elk permit for the Shoshone National Forest, I had also drawn an antelope permit for the Casper area through which we were driving. A map of my assigned area had been furnished with the license, but neither of us could read it very well. We decided to stop in the first town and ask for help.

The first town consisted of a half dozen houses, three windmills pumping oil, and a saloon. We went into the saloon which was occupied by two cowboys drinking whiskey, a young woman dressed like John Wayne's girlfriend, and the bartender.

I ordered two whiskeys and put a $20 bill on the bar and got my first of many surprises way out west. My change consisted of 18 silver dollars. People didn't seem to trust paper money in those days. The bartender couldn't figure out my map either, but advised me to drive out of town and shoot the first buck with a nice set of horns which is exactly what I did. I passed up the first buck, who was running with a bunch of does, but the second bunch was just ambling along and the buck had a big head.

Instead of taking off after they saw us all six animals stopped to stare, and I took time to sit and climb into my rifle sling before squeezing off a shot at a 50-yard target.

I dressed out the antelope in five minutes and we stopped by at the saloon before heading out to the Wind River.

However, while shooting the antelope had been easy, I learned during my first week of hunting in the mountains that elk are hard to come by. Tripp had a base camp in the Shoshone forest 40 miles above Dubois which could be reached by truck from Dubois. In 1956 every party hunted by horseback from the base camp although Tripp also had a couple of spike camps reached only by horseback from the base camp.

During my first week I had glimpses of a few elk in the forest. I also saw a number of mule deer, all does, and a bull, cow and calf moose. But even though I didn't fire all week I enjoyed the daily hunts. Mostly we hunted from horseback, stopping frequently to dismount and glass the country for game.

At the end of the week our six-man party broke camp for the truck ride back to Dubois. We had taken four elk, two of them bulls, and one mule deer. I had nothing. Having used up all of the time I had planned to hunt I had all intentions of heading back for New Jersey and home on Sunday. We got back to Dubois on Friday and I had the rest of that day and all of Saturday to kill.

Mrs. Tripp was the first person to start changing my plans about going home. When I got to the ranch kitchen she said to me, "Hank, I don't think you like it very well out here." Surprised, I asked her why?

She answered, "well you've only been in Wyoming a week and a half. You haven't gotten that bull elk you had your heart set on and now you want to go back home." I told her that getting the bull really didn't matter, that I'd be back another season and probably do better.

To be sure I was deeply disappointed about not getting an elk, but hated to admit it. Ina (Mrs. Tripp) said, why don't you go to town tomorrow night and go back hunting with another party on Sunday? I still had a week's vacation time left and I really didn't have to terminate my trip so soon.

Tempted, I told her that I would telephone my wife from Dubois Saturday night and if she agreed, I would stay for another week. Bob Tripp, who had come into the kitchen while Ina and I were talking and who had overhead the conversation, said "your wife will tell you to come back home, that you've been gone long enough. She will tell you that she misses you, that the kids miss you, and that you'd better be back home and pronto."

I told Tripp he didn't know my wife very well. She might just a gree that I should stay for another try to get an elk. I fished for brown and rainbow trout in the Wind River on Friday evening and Saturday morning, and successfully too.

The following night, freshly shaven and showered and feeling great I borrowed one of Tripp's pick-up trucks and headed into Dubois and the every-Saturday-night blast. It was the only town in a very vast region and on Saturday night the saloons with their dance halls and game tables attracted cowboys and cowgals from as far as 200 miles. In addition to the whites there were many Indians from the big reservation south of Dubois.

The festive crowd drank, smoked, gambled, danced and raised hell all night long. Sunday morning invariably got off to a slow start. During the course of Saturday night I telephoned my wife from one of the saloons, telling her of the Tripps' suggestion that I stay on for another week.

Lillian said, "well you went primarily to try to get a bull elk. Why don't you stay? A mounted elk head would make a fine trophy for the hall."

That is all I wanted to hear.

Next morning after breakfast in Dubois' only restaurant, late opening on Sundays, I headed back to base camp in the Shoshone Forest with Don Spears, who had been my guide the first week; a couple of other guides and the wrangler, a young fellow from Oregon.

Once again I was going to hunt with Spears. The other hunter was a young man from Pennsylvania who had never been elk hunting before. In fact I don't think he had much experience with any type of hunting. We hunted for three days and my luck was exactly the same as it had been the previous week. I saw no elk and only a few deer, none with antlers.

On the fourth day the three of us rode into a huge open park surrounded by jagged mountains. Grass grew profusely on the level valley floor. There was the inevitable crystaline trout stream bubbling through the middle of the valley.

Soon after riding into the park we heard a shrill whistle from a mountain top high to our left. It was the first time in my life that I had heard an elk bugle and I was disappointed. It sounded to me like a kid blowing on a whistle instead of the much more noble sound that I had expected an elk would make.

Spears, on the lead horse, stopped and looked up. I think that if he had been alone he would have tied his horse, climbed that mountain on foot, and try to shoot the elk. However, with two dudes in tow, he had to keep riding.

Later, on higher ground, where the valley was quite narrow, Spears left the other hunter to stand on watch, and then he and I rode along the bank of the stream. Eventually we tied our horses to some trees growing on the edge of a little glade, and sat down to look and listen.

Within minutes, and from what seemed to be the very top of a forbidding looking sheer high wall of rock to the west came the now familiar sound of a bull elk bugling. We were at 8,000 feet above sea level and the elk was at the edge of tree line at 10,000 feet. The mountain where he was was so steep I marvelled that any trees at all were able to grow on its side.

So there was a bull elk right above me and all I had to do was climb a rock wall of 2,000 feet to get to where he was. Spears asked me if I was game for the climb and of course I was just raring to go. Because we knew that the climb was going to be difficult we decided to carry only our rifles.

I had my old Winchester Model 54 bolt action .30/06 which was fitted with a four-power telescope. Spears carried a lever-action .30/30. For a while we climbed together but then came to a sheer wall of rock that neither man nor beast could scale. The sharply tilted spruce and pine grew to either side of the wall.

While we stood there, panting, wondering what to do, the elk bugled again high above. It was impossible to tell whether a climb to the left or right of the wall would get us closest to the bull. I suggested that Spears take one side I the other. The camp cook, his girl friend, had an unfilled elk license and I knew that he was out to try to get an elk for her.

Spears, happy to be on his own, chose the slope to the right of the rock wall and I went up the other. I was 46 years old and in fine shape.

With the rifle strapped to my back, I climbed that mountain by grabbing for every root, sapling and stone; digging my toes into and over every crack. I thought my lungs would burst or my heart would stop. I was almost afraid to look back down. From time to time I looked to the mountains on the opposite side of the valley to judge how much farther I would have to climb to reach timber line.

I wanted to quit a score of times, sure that no elk could possibly live on a slope so steep, but every time that bull would blow his whistle again. At length I came to a dry arroyo on the face of the mountain. It had been cut by snow, rock and tree slides. It resembled a dry stream bed running straight up and down the mountain.

Stunted trees grew on both sides of the arroyo. I continued to climb, now along the edge of the arroyo, fighting for every foot of altitude and determined to reach tree line even if my lungs did burst.

I had given up all hope of ever seeing the elk.

Suddenly, possibly a half mile away, to my right, and at the same elevation, I heard a shot. Then I heard several more. I was both highly elated and most deeply disappointed. I knew that Spears had seen the elk and I was sure that he had killed it and I was happy for him and for his girl friend. At the same time I was feeling extremely sorry for myself.

I was sure that I had failed, and doubted that I would ever get an elk. Nevertheless, I determined to keep climbing. I was sure timberline couldn't be more than a few hundred yards higher.

And then I heard something crashing through the trees. Whatever it was, it ws coming along the side of the mountain above me and to the right. I've heard a lot of noisy animals in my time, but I never heard another animal making as much noise as that big bull elk.

Spears hadn't killed him after all. He had seen him rubbing his huge antlers against a tree on the far side of a wide rock slide and had fired several shots at it. But the range was long and all he had succeeded in doing was to scare it.

The bull burst into view from the scrubby growth about 75 yards away and at about an 80 degree angle above me. It looked higher than a mountain and its four legs were pumping like the pistons of an old steam locomotive. The bull was just about to cross the arroyo directly above me when I fired the first shot.

This climb had started in early afternoon and the sun was now dipping over the top of the moutain. Its rays through the scope nearly blinded me and I could just about make out the elk. I aimed the middle of the telescope at the chest area of the bull, pulled the trigger and hoped for the best.

The bull staggered but plunged down the bank of the arroyo and leaped to reach the opposite bank. He was in slightly better light now and I could see him clearly through the glass. I fired again at his chest. The elk crashed to the rocky ground and started tumbling and rolling down the arroyo, picking up a ton of rocks, stones, broken branches and litter as he came.

He rolled down that arroyo like a giant basketball, end over end, and boulders as big as basketballs rolled with him. It started a veritable landslide but magically the bull stopped rolling when he was only about 25 feet from me. The rest of the landslide, several tons of it, kept roaring down the steep slope, the rocks bouncing down the mountain like rubber balls.

The noise was incredible.

The bull was nearly dead now. He tried to raise his head but with two bullets through the chest and an avalanche for a coup de grace he was through. Miraculously, I thought, the fine rack was not harmed. He had five points on one side and six on the other.

He was a fine looking bull and I couldn't have been happier.

I sat on a boulder close to that bull, resting and trying to regain my composure. Spears, who had heard me shoot of course, had also heard the landslide and wasn't quite sure whether he would find me alive or dead.

He came along on the same route the elk had taken, about a half hour later. Without an axe we had one awful time working on that elk but finally we got the hind quarters off by severing the spine and flesh just above them.

Spears kicked the hindquarters down the mountain. They bounded down the steep slope like a pair of giant pants. I carried the head and cape, falling frequently and why I didn't get hurt I'll never know.

Spears with the elk hindquarters and I with the head arrived back at the little clearing close to sundown. We hung the quarters and propped up the head. Then we got our horses and rode off to pick up the other hunter.

We had been gone for so long he was badly frightened and worried that he would have to spend the night in the woods. As it was it was very late and very dark when we rode back into camp that night.

But I was the happiest man in the world.

# Horse Sense

All my life I had read and heard that if you ever get lost all you have to do is give your horse free rein and he will get you home. I didn't know whether the story was true or not, but on one memorable occasion I had a chance to test it.

This was in the Shoshone National Forest in the Wind River Range of Wyoming in 1956. I had been in camp nearly two weeks and the guides had the idea that I was beginning to know the area fairly well. Actually I thought so too although I had never set out for a day of hunting alone and I had never been compelled to find my way back to camp.

During this trip I usually rode a big gelding named Dusty who was almost the exact color of an elk. I guess you would say the color was yellowish brown. It used to bother me because I thought that someday some anxious-to-score sport might mistake Dusty for an elk and hit the horse or rider.

However, Dusty was a good strong horse and we got along well, on the whole. He never got saddle sores, or lame, and always seemed to be ready and anxious to work. So I rode him just about every day.

He didn't get nervous in the high places and would pick up tufts of grass or twigs as he walked along, even on the edge of a precipice with a 1,000-foot drop. Once, with me aboard, he decided to leap over a narrow ravine to save the climb down one side and up the other.

His leap carried us over the heads of two or three dismounted riders and their steeds who were in the process of negotiating the ravine by the more sensible method. The men thought it had been my idea to leap the chasm. The idea was strictly Dusty's.

However, everybody thought I was very brave, or crazy.

Then one day I became lost. It was mid afternoon. Guide Don Spears and I had been riding together. He said he was going to pick up another hunter who had been left alone to keep vigil for elk on some high basins. Spears told me to meet him at the juncture of two trails that I knew well. I agreed and rode off alone.

It was a beautiful October afternoon, clear and sunny, and the mountains were magnificent. I thought I'd take a shortcut through a dense forest instead of sticking to the trail. The forest was much larger than I had imagined and when I emerged into open country on the other side I didn't recognize any of the mountains.

I wasn't worried yet but as I rode on, continually coming to the edges of cliffs or precipices that I did not recognize I became more and more concerned.

After an hour or so, riding in an area I was sure I had never seen before, I knew I was lost. The sun was dropping. I knew camp was somewhere to the southwest but in the Rocky Mountains it isn't simple to stear a straight and simple course. There might be a mountain in the way.

If there was ever a time to test the homing instinct of a horse, this was the time. I let the reins go slack, nudged Dusty in the ribs and told him to go home.

The big gelding started off at a trot, almost immediately leaving the old game trail we were on and plunging into heavy pine woods. It was already dark in the woods and to keep from being brushed off the horse's back I leaned forward over his neck.

Dusty travelled steadily through one stand of trees after another. He walked or strotted along the edges of cliffs, plunged down and up precipitous trails, crossed brooks, and wound his way through and around windfalls.

Steadily it became darker. Then we travelled in nearly total darkness in open country, and total in the forest. There was no moon but the stars lit up the landscape, dimly, in the open.

The horse seemed to know where he was going and I was confident we'd wind up somewhere, but I wondered if Dusty was headed for our camp in the mountains or was going back to his ranch, wherever that might be. Dubois was the nearest town and that was some 40 miles from camp.

My outfitter was Bob Tripp and his Red Rock ranch was 20 miles south of Dubois. I couldn't even imagine where in relation to Dubois Dusty's home ranch might be.

My worries were interrupted by a pack of coyottes which broke into blood curdling cries within 100 yards. The wild chorus made no impression upon Dusty but I was scared white.

After the coyottes stopped yelping I rode on in silence. Dusty was now walking steadily and I knew we were in open country. I sensed that he was on a trail of some sort. Four hours had elapsed since the time I had given the big horse his head and it seemed longer than that.

I was thinking about the coyottes when I detected ghostly white shapes to my left. I was all ready to be scared again when I realized what they were. They were the outer tents, next to the big corral, back at camp.

We were home!

The horses in the corral whinnied a greeting and Dusty snorted and whinnied back. Never had I been so relieved to dismount. I unsaddled Dusty and rubbed him down. I got his feed bag and gave him an extra large can of oats before turning him into the corral.

Then I took my rifle and other gear up to my tent and went into the cook tent. Mable, our cook, was surprised to see me. She said, "you're the first one back. Where are the others?"

I told her I thought they would be along after a while. It took nearly an hour for the rest of the crew to get to camp. "How come you're here so long?" asked Spears.

I told him I had taken a short cut and he and the others were much impressed. I never told them what had actually happened.

Moments after the picture, Capt. George Burlew dropped the leader after the eight-foot white marlin had been brought close to the boat the first time. The author is the man on the rod.

# White Marlin

Ocean City, Maryland , was "the white marlin capital of the world" in 1960 when Finn H. Magnus of Essex Fells and Manasquan, N.J. started exploring the Hudson Canyon with a 50-foot sports fishing boat designed specifically for the purpose.

She was powered by two 235 HP GM diesels that drove her at more than 20 knots, and her tanks held 540 gallons of diesel fuel, enough for a 10-day voyage. In addition to radar and sonar she had a Loran A, the first one I ever saw. There were three fighting chairs in the roomy cockpit, sleeping accommodations for 10, a stove, refrigerator and even a shower.

There was also a sit-down electric organ. Magnus, who made his first fortune manufacturing harmonicas, made his second making electric organs.

Magnus' first captain had been Johnny Harms of Stuart, Florida, a noted big game fishing guide who operated the first boat during the harmonica years. But in 1960 he depended largely on the expertise of Capt. George Burlew of Manasquan, also one of the best in the business. He was a master at rigging balao and mullet baits for marlin.

At that time the Texas Tower still stood guard near the inshore edge of the canyon, and it was there that the yacht Mangus would lie at anchor each night. The tower looked like an impregnable fortress and no one would have believed that someday it would be destroyed by a storm, and that a lot servicemen would die.

The outer edges of the Continental Shelf were actively being fished by commercial boats during the 1950s both for finfish and lobsters, but the sports fishing boats out of Long Island, N.Y., and Monmouth and Ocean counties in New Jersey seldom ventured more than 20 miles off shore.

They didn't have to travel far in those days.

Starting the last week in June and continuing through July bluefin tuna would be migrating along the beaches, to be followed by bonito, skipjack and false albacore, although everybody called them just plain albacore at that time.

The word tuna was never prefixed by bluefin, because nobody knew that there were other tuna species off the New Jersey shore. That is nobody but some commercial fishermen who knew that there were a lot of strange gamefish out on the shelf, even if they didn't know exactly what they were.

For the most part the commercial fishermen at Point Pleasant and Point Pleasant Beach were Scandinavians, mostly Swedes and Norwegians, who didn't have much truck with the gentlemen members of the Brielle Marlin and Tuna Club and the Manasquan River Marlin and Tuna Club who owned their own boats.

Magnus, however, was different. He was an immigrant from Denmark who never lost his accent, and who was not above hobnobbing with fishermen in smelly clothes. They took him under their wings, told him what they thought was out on the shelf, and Magnus went about designing his second and last super sports fishing boat.

During his first season on the Hudson Canyon Magnus brought back more white marlin than all of the other boats combined, 200 pound tuna, the first true albacore ever seen at Brielle, a number of spearfish, dolphin, and other species.

In 1962 Magnus invited several outdoor writers to make a trip with him, including myself, who had never caught a marlin either off New Jersey or Maryland. The rule aboard the charter boats was to keep hands off the tackle until the mate had coaxed a fish to take a bait and had it firmly hooked.

Then the rod was turned over to whoever in the party wanted to "catch" the fish. Hooking a marlin on a rigged bait was the most difficult part of the operation by far, and I never wanted to play a fish that someone else had hooked.

On the trip on the Magnus we trolled the rim of the canyon one entire day and failed to raise a fish. We saw nothing and didn't get a strike. That night we slept near the tower, and resumed trolling the following morning.

It looked like a repeat of the day before, and the rest of the group whiled away the time in the cabins, while Burlew and I rode on the bridge and watched the four baits in the water. Two were trailing from the outriggers 40 feet aft, and two on the flat lines from holders in the stern.

I had fished with Burlew for giant tuna off Nova Scotia, Maine, Montauk and of course New Jersey, and knew that he hated sharks and refused to fish for them.

I asked him why and then, for the first time, he told me of that awful day in the summer of 1916 when a white shark killed two people in Matawan Creek, New Jersey, eight miles up from the ocean.

Burlew, who was born in Keyport in 1897, lived close to the creek in Matawan in 1916. The creek is tidal, deep enough for naviagation, and at that time barges loaded with bricks from a local factory were towed from there to New York City.

On July 12, the day of the tragedy, Stanley Fisher who lived next door burst into Burlew's house with the news that a shark had just attacked a young swimmer and that the boy had disappeared. The boy was Lester Stillwell.

Burlew and Fisher ran to the creek to join a crowd of frightened people who were staring at the bloody water. There was no sign of the boy and no sign of the shark.

The two men decided that the thing to do was to don swimming trunks and dive to try to retrieve the body. The creek at that point is 35 feet wide and 18 feet deep. They dived a number of times and swam for about a half hour without finding anything and with no sign of the shark.

Then they decied to rest near the opposite bank, standing in waist deep water. Fisher told Burlew that he didn't think there was any use in continuing the search and the latter agreed. Then both struck out again, intending to cross the creek and change back into their clothes.

They were half way across the creek when Burlew felt the water starting to churn alongside him, and in the next instant his companion screamed.

"Stanley was a big man, weighing 200 pounds, and he fought back at the shark, striking it with his fists," said Burlew. "He was fighting desperately to break away from the shark, striking and kicking at it with all his might.

"Three or four times during the struggle the shark pulled him under water, but each time he got back to the surface. Finally Stanley managed to work himself free of the monster and resumed swimming toward shore. It was not until he reached the bank and tried to walk that he realized that the shark had bitten a huge chunk from the upper portion of one leg."

"The bite extended from just above the knee almost to the hip. Just about half of the thigh was missing, " said Burlew.

He fell into silence after that, and I didn't have anything to say either. Fisher died in the hospital eight hours after he left the water and remains of the boy's body were recovered four days later.

For a long time we just sat staring at the baits in an ocean that seemed to be devoid of all life, when suddenly there were simultaneous explosive strikes at both of the outrigger baits, and people re-appeared like magic in the cockpit.

The bait on the port side had disappeared and Magnus yanked th rod out of the holder and struck to set the hook. The fish was on, but only for a few minutes, and Magnus kept holding the rod and talking to the others nearby.

I saw that the bait on the starboard was in plain view, but barely moving since the engines were disengaged. I missed most of the ladder rungs getting to the deck and yanked the rod from the holder.

With reel in free spool I started pumping the rod to give the bait some movement and within seconds a shadow appeared, materializing into a marlin that opened its jaws, and the bait disappeared inside. The marlin turned in slow motion and settled out of sight.

The line was running off steadily and I flipped the lever, and when the line tightened I struck. In an instant the marlin flung himself 12 feet above the water and then tore away on its first long run.

I had him up to the boat within 15 minutes, but when Burlew grabbed the leader the marlin made another dash for freedom and Burlew promptly dropped the leader which was exactly the right thing to do.

Many boatmen, once they have their gloved hands on the leader refuse to let go and even ask for help to drag the fish in. Burlew was never like that and as far as I know he never broke a leader on a fish that was just starting to fight.

A half hour later I had the marlin back at the boat and this time Burlew held the leader and young Kenneth Magnus gaffed him. He was eight feet long and weighed 87 pounds.

The marlin was mounted by the late Fred Huber of Belmar who was an excellent painter as well as an outstanding taxidermist.

Burlew, who died in Florida in the spring of 1987 at the age of 90, had his own charter boat at Brielle and for many years was captain of several fishing yachts owned by Maurice and Carolyn Meyer of Elberon, N.J.

In all, there were four people killed by sharks in 1916 along the New Jersey shore and according to Jack Casey all four may have been caused by the same fish. Casey is the author of Anglers' Guide to Sharks who is now stationed at the Narragansett, R.I. laboratory of the U.S. Fish and Wildlife Service.

The first attack was "just before the Fourth of July" when Charles Epping Van Sant, 23, Philadelphia, went swimming in the surf off Center Street, Beach Heven. A shark attacked him and "horribly mangled one leg." He was pulled out of the water by U.S. Olympic swimmer Alexander Ott but died on the way to the hospital in Toms River.

The second attack occurred "five days later" when Charles Bruder "went for his customary afternoon swim at Spring Lake." He was employed at the hotels there and was a good swimmer.

He was beyond the safety rope when the shark attacked. Lifeguards

Chris Anderson and George White went out in their boat and pulled Bruder aboard, "but both of his lower limbs were virtually gone. The man was dead before the boat got back to the beach."

Then came the twin killings in Matawan Creek by a monster which had to enter Raritan Bay and pass Keyport before ascending the creek.

A newspaper story in the Matawan Journal on July 13, 1916 said that Arthur Smith of Matawan also dove for the body of Lester Stillwell, and according to Jeffrey Pfeiffer of Jackson, Smith's great grandson, the shark attacked him too.

On the morning of July 14, 1916, a trawler captured an eight-and-a-half-foot white shark in Raritan Bay. It had "15 pounds of human remains" in its belly.

There were no further attacks reported and this may have been the end of the rogue shark, if indeed only one was responsible.

# The Farm Pond

Happiness is a clear, spring fed farm pond containing a self perpetuating population of largemouth bass thriving on an ample forage base of rock and calico bass, frogs and minnows. But for five years the star performer in Joe and Ben Dressner's pond was a northern pike.

It was caught several times each season, always on live bait and always carefully released. It was frequently sighted in the shallows close to shore, and while it would stalk plugs, spinners and spoons it never struck one.

After all, striking an artificial lure had cost it its liberty in the first place, and the big fish never forgot. The last time one of the boys caught it it was about 28 inches long, a beautiful fish.

And then it disappeared.

The farm is in Ontario County, New York, and Joe and Ben were just little kids when they first moved there with their parents Dr. Steve and Betty Dressner. Their sister Sue wasn't even born yet. Their father was chief surgeon in the Clifton Springs Hospital and didn't have much time for fishing, but the boys fished the pond every day after school, and Saturdays and Sundays.

The former owners of the farm had stocked the pond with fingerling rainbow trout and the Dressners followed suit. They bought several hundred rainbow fingerlings, some of which managed to reach six inches by the following year, a project that was far from an outstanding success.

When wife Lillian and I first visited daughter Betty and grandsons Joseph, 10; and Benjamin, 8, the pond still had the year-old rainbows in it, and I suggested that we stock it with rock bass and black crappies as forage, and largemouth bass for fun and food.

Everybody agreed and all hands started fishing for creatures to stock the pond. We caught more smallmouths than largemouths and while the former didn't reproduce they grew to three pounds. The three other species produced swarms of offspring all of which grew to large size.

It was on one of those pond stocking expeditions that we caught the pike under rather strange circumstances, but that fish taught all of us a lot, especially grandpa.

We had gone to fish in the huge pool formed below the long spillway from the Lake Ontario barge canal near the town of Newark. The pool is inhabited by many species, smallmouth and largemouth bass, walleyes, northern pike and swarms of black crappies.

It was the crappies or calico bass that we were interested in, or rather that Ben and I were interested in. Joe was interested in casting for pike with a big spinning outfit, using all of the allegedly deadly pike lures in grandpa's big tackle box.

He failed to draw a strike.

But Ben and I were using ultra-light spinning tackle, baiting with inch and a half fathead minnows and catching one calico bass after the other. We used small cork floats to keep the minnows above the rocky bottom and every five minutes or so our floats would go under to signalize the arrival of another little bass.

Soon we had about a dozen crappies in our water filled cooler which we used for our fish stocking tank and then the action stopped. We were puzzled, but after a while my float went under again, but when I struck I found that instead of another crappie I had a two-foot northern pike hooked.

The pike cut my four-pound test line in a matter of moments and we continued fishing, but it soon became obvious that the school of crappies had been routed by the pike.

Joe continued to cast for pike with 12-pound test line, but without success. So we left to stock the dozen crappies in the farm pond.

The next morning we were back with another supply of little minnows. The first time my cork went down I felt nothing when I tried to set the hook. I retrieved my line minus the hook and minnow and knew that the pike was back.

Minutes later Benny hooked the pike and had it on for several minutes before it cut the line. I determined to catch that thieving pike, and borrowing Joe's big outfit tried all of the regulation pike lures in the tackle box.

Nothing.

I hadn't been paying attention to the boys. Since they were very small they never hesitated to take whatever they wanted from grandpa's tackle box. I was back at the box, with my back to the water, searching for some lure that might work, when I heard Joe yell, "get the net grandpa I've got the pike."

He did indeed. Two feet of thrashing pike was on the surface and I soon had it safely in the net.

The lure Joe used had me dumbfounded. It was a Tin Liz, an aluminum stamping of a fish with a hinged metal tail and an single No. 10 hook. This painted one-and-a-half inch spoon was once fairly popular for trout, but I would never have used it to try to catch a pike.

It had been in my tackle box, unused, for perhaps 25 years, but children don't know that in order tot catch big pike they have to use big lures.

But do they?

Going over the events of the two days it finaly dawned on me that that pike had been feeding on very small fish, selectively, like a trout on midges that shows no interest in larger flies that it might take at another time.

The pike that took the midget lure was the only fish we had in the water filled cooler. It was in an oblique position because it was too long to fit along th side.

It wasn't too hard to convince the boys that we should quit fishing and transport the pike to the farm pond to join all of the other fish. We released it in a shallow end but after a while it swam out and vanished in the depths.

Weeks passed before it was seen again, but then it seemed to become accustomed to people, like boys and girls trying to catch it.

Once or twice a year it was brought to net, and always released again.

Ben, Joe and friends caught it several times and Betty had it hooked, but I never did. Perhaps I should have tried the Tin Liz.

A good eight pointer on the Kittatinny Ridge in Warren County.

# The Deer In The River

The temperature hovered at five degrees above zero in the snow covered woods of East Hanover, New Jersey the fourth day of the deer season in 1958. I had spent the first day of the season along the Delaware River in Warren County but had seen no bucks. I had left to go to work on the second day and a heavy snowfall had prevented my driving the 75 miles from my home in Livingston to Warren County where I had intended to hunt the fourth day.

So, at 7 a.m., there I was in the bitterly cold woods near my home hoping, feebly, for a shot. I was deathly still. As far as I could tell there wasn't another hunter in the woods, no one to push a deer my way. I tried sitting in a tree stand for a while, but it was much too cold.

Then I tried short walks to keep my blood circulating, and standing to watch and wait. I saw nothing. I heard nothing. I had left my car at the cemetery of East Hanover and had travelled about a mile to the south and east and was near to the Passaic River which I was sure was solidly frozen over.

I had not seen a single fresh deer track.

By 10 a.m. I decided that I had had enough. Since there didn't appear to be any deer in the area that morning and since there were no other hunters (I thought) anywhere else to move them around, I figured I'd give up and go home.

So I trudged steadily through the powder light six inch snow in the direction of the car. I had gone about a half mile when I heard crackling in the thick brush to my left my first thought was that it was caused by another hunter.

I didn't even slow down but looked to catch a glimpse of the man. It wasn't a man. The crackling had been caused by deer, seven of them, all in wild flight and now speeding rapidly away. One, running right in the middle of the group, was a handsome full-racked buch.

I was sick. Had I been pussyfooting along, instead of trudging, I might have gotten close enough to the buck to get a shot. Instead I had simply stampeded the entire herd.

Disconsolately, I started to follow the tracks of the running deer, convinced that I would never see them again, but for the moment I had forgotten about going home.

Then the strangest thing happened. From far away in the woods, in the direction in which the deer had disappeared, I heard a tinkling sound. Instantly I guessed what it was. The herd had crossed the ice of the river and the flying hooves had broken a thin crust.

So what? The deer were gone.

I wandered over to a tree and put my back against its trunk. I just stood there, thinking about what a fool I had been. It was just as cold as ever but I wasn't feeling it any more. There wasn't much of a breeze but from time to time it came in from the direction of the river.

I thought I heard ice tinkling but put the thought down to imagination. However, I found myself straining to hear. Soon the sounds came again, ever so faintly, and suddenly it hit me. If the sounds were really caused by breaking ice one or more of the deer must be in the river.

I started to run but then walked. I knew that if a deer had really broken through the ice and was in the river it would not be able to get out and there wasn't much I could do about it.

There is a steep bank along the west side of the Passaic in Hanover. I could not see the river until I was almost on top of it. The deer had taken the river from that high bank and the tracks of the herd had gone through heavy growth. The branches of a downed tree further obscured my view of the river.

So I was directly on the top of the bank before I saw what I hope never to see again. In the middle of the frozen river, some 60 feet wide at that point, was a 10-foot wide hole of water. In the hole, swimming in circles aound the edge, was the buck, a seven pointer.

The rest of the herd had crossed safely. The heaviest deer had fallen through and he was doomed. Time after time he got his forelegs out of the hole, but hooves are no substitute for hands and fingers.

He couldn't crawl out.

Two bucks and two does in Woodlands near Morristown, New Jersey.

I did not want to shoot the deer. I wanted to get him out of the hole, but I had no intention of going out on the ice after him. I didn't want to join him in the water. I knew that if he had broken through I would too.

So, helpless, I watched from the high bank. During the next half hour, which seemed like an eternity, I watched that deer. He was tiring. The cold and the exertion were killing him.

At last, unable to watch him struggle any more, I trained the bead of the shotgun on his neck and fired. Buckshot pellets slammed into him, some spattering the water above and below his neck. He was still alive. I fired again and he was still.

He floated to the downstream side of the hole and I waited for the current to carry the carcass under the ice and out of sight forever. But the shoulders remained afloat, jutting several inches above the top of the ice.

I stood there for a long while. The brown form remained. It didn't look like any part of a deer, just a brown form.

I worked out a plan. The bank on the east, Livingston, side of the river, was gently sloping. The river was shallower there. Perhaps I could work my way out to the deer from the east bank. Determined to try I promptly left the river bank and walked back through the woods and to my car, passing two other hunters on the way. I told them nothing.

Back home I told my wife what had happened and she agreed to my plan to get the deer. She donned boots and warm clothing and we drove to the first bridge north of the deer, parking next to Flynn's Tavern on the Livingston side. On the half mile journey south along the river bank Lillian, my wife, fell several times on snow covered ice but was not injured.

When, at long last, we got to the scene, nothing had changed much except that now several points of the buck's antlers were visible. I had brought a rope and an axe and tried chopping my way out to the deer but to no avail.

At length I cut 15 feet off the rope, to make a lariat, then tied one end of the rest of it around my waist. With the rope around my waist I started walking out to the hole, very slowly, with Lillian on shore holding on to the other end of the rope.

As I got nearer the deer the ice began to creak and sag. I got on my belly and wormed my way closer to the deer. Water commenced pouring from the hole and soon I was lying in water, still moving closer to the deer. I was scared.

I was never much of a hand at throwing a lariat and trying to toss a loop over that deer's antlers, while prone, was a feat I hope never to have to do again. After about the 50th toss, miraculously, the loop dropped over a fork in the antlers and with trembling fingers I tightened it.

Slowly I pulled the head of the deer to my side of the hole and then grabbed the antlers with both hands. With Lillian pulling me and me pulling the deer I worked the head and neck out of the hole.

Getting that buck's shoulders above the ice was one of the hardest jobs I have ever had to do in my life. Once the shoulders were out, the rest was easy. The deer was drawn entirely out of the hole. With Lillian still tugging at me with the rope I slid that deer safely to shore.

I dressed the deer promptly. My wet clothes on my chest, belly and legs, were now frozen but I didn't care. Lillian and I dragged that deer to the car in triumph and loaded him into the back seat. Nobody had seen us park. Nobody had seen us walk off into the woods, and nobody saw us bring the deer back to the car.

There were hunters there but they were all in the tavern.

# The Ten Pointer

Starting about 1950 and for a period of more than 15 years the deer hunting in an area of what is now the Tocks Island National Recreation Area was excellent. The specific area I am writing about was owned and/or leased by the Coventry Hunting Club in Pahaquarry Township of Warren County, New Jersey. The southern end of the property was in the area of the old Copper Mine Inn and extended from there to the area of Millbrook, bounded on the west by the Delaware River and on the east by the Appalachian Trail along the Kittatinny Mountain Range.

At one time the lowlands were farmed but during the period of which I am writing farming had largely disappeared. The fields remained but instead of corn and other vegetable crops they now grew mostly grass. With the end of farming wild pheasants disappeared and the best of the shooting was for game farm pheasants. The Coventry Hunting Club stocked up to 1,500 pheasants each fall, just before the season and on Fridays and Sundays during the season. No hunting was permitted on those two days.

Other small game hunting on the Coventry tract, roughly 4,000 acres, was best for squirrels, good for woodcock, poor to fair for ruffed grouse and poor for cottontails.

If there was anything wrong with the deer hunting at Coventry it was that the woods were too lightly hunted. Because fees were charged for hunting privileges at Coventry there were never as many men in the woods there as in the large state-owned Worthington Tract directly south of the club controlled lands.

At Coventry hunting pressure was largely on the opening day Monday and the Saturday closing day of the annual six-day season. Back in the days when the herds were at their peak at Coventry it was not unusual to see 50 deer on the first day of the season and none or only a few on subsequent days until Saturday. There simply would not be enough men in the woods to move the game.

For a decade, during this period, a group of us leased a small cabin for the deer season. The cabin had a combination living and dining room heated, after a fashion, by a wood or coal burning stove; a kitchenette with a bottle gas burning stove; two small unheated bedrooms and a bathroom with broken plumbing.

There was a cellar and a front porch that extended the length of the house. The old bunch that hunted there included Jack, Stanley and Jules Bystrak of the Chatham area family, frequently their brother Walter, always Don Schulte of Livingston; their sons and Schulte's daughter, and myself. We moved in the day before the season and those of us who could hunted the entire week.

Success was good. Everybody got deer, although not every man got a buck every season. We killed some deer by driving, frequently resorting to this method after the first day of the season when for the most part we had the woods to ourselves. The Kittatinny Range is a rough one and the slopes are long and hard to clumb. The terrain discourages nearly all but the most ambitious hunters.

After shooting an excellent eight-point head in Pennsylvania right in back of the house in 1959, I came to the conclusion that I had been running around the woods to much and wandering too far from camp.

Since deer were as plentiful in the area of camp as anywhere within a day's walk away I decided to spend more time on watch and less time walking. Accordingly, I selected what I thought would be a good stand close to the cabin.

I picked a dandy. It was within a quarter mile of the cabin, on a knoll up the slope northwards from camp. My stand was on the ground in the branches of a downed tree. One branch served for a very comfortable seat and another served as a foot rest. I had a clearing in the center for my fire. Branches of the dead tree served to break up my profile. I addition, I laid other saplings around my seat, in tepee fashion, to give an over-all appearance, according to Don Schulte, of a "beaver house."

I fixed up my stand before the season, laying in a generous supply of

**No antlers on any of these deer, which were feeding unafraid on an estate near Madison, N.J.**

firewood. The first season I used it was in 1960 and I shot a spike buck there. I shot the buck on the opposite side of the stand as I was hiking up a slope to it. Range was 40 yards. This was in a deep snow that had fallen during a severe storm the following day and most of the night.

The following season, on dry gournd, and also on the first day of the season, I shot a buck while seated in the stand. This was also a spike and range was 65 yards. My stand was actually on fire at the time the buck appeared, walking, and I shot right through the flames. During those years I was using my old World War II Remington made Browning Automatic with 30-inch full choke Remington barrel and loaded with Haelig 000 buckshot.

The year 1962 was the all time banner year for deer hunting at Coventry and, for that matter, the entire north Jersey area. The state, determined to prune herds considered overly large in many areas, was generous in the issuance of party permits valid during the season.

A single permit was available for four-man parties which allowed the taking of a fifth deer of either sex in addition to the up to four bucks they were entitled to.

I started the festivities with a 10 pointer, a beautiful buck which I did not weigh. However, he was a very large animal and the head would have made a fine trophy.

As in 1961, we had snow, but only about a foot of powder compared to the more than two feet we had had then. I had tramped to my stand before the legal starting time of 7 a.m. I had brushed the snow from my seat and covered it with a cushion. I had my gun propped up within reach and started my fire. The smoke billowed around me and through the leaned saplings and branches of my tepee.

Conscious of the party permit I was determined to shoot the first deer that came by. After about an hour I saw a hunter climbing the old jeep trail leading up the mountain north of my stand. He stopped to rest on the very spot where, the previous year, the spike buck had appeared, the one I shot that season.

This man stood in plain sight only 65 yards away. I thought he would stand there forever, but after a half hour he began walking again, going higher on the trail and wandered out of sight.

He hadn't been out of sight for more than five minutes when I heard several shots from the area where I guessed he should have been and within moments a herd of a dozen or more deer came bounding down through the woods and right at me.

The entire herd was zeroed in right at my tepee and within a moment deer were bounding by me, some to the left and some to the right, and none more than 30 feet away. I tried to shoot one, any one, but my gun barrel hit a sapling of my tepee and I couldn't get lined up on a single one.

**Jim Lucadema of Maplewood hunted successfully from this safe and comfortable stand he built near his camp in Beaver Brook, Sullivan County, New York.**

In other words, I missed the entire herd but I shot the gun anyhow, maybe three times for all I know. If the deer had come by farther out from my stand and especially if they had been moving more slowly I would certainly have killed one of them. As it was they burst almost right on top of me and instead of hitting a deer I simply banged the barrel of my long gun against a pole.

Mortified, I stepped out of my stand and started to follow the tracks of the departed herd. I looked for blood but was sure I wouldn't find any. Up until then I had always argued that it was impossible to completely miss a deer with buckshot within 50 yards.

I had missed an entire herd at within 30 feet.

Feeling glum I decided to walk after the herd for a while. The deer had run down the steep slope and then turned south to follow relatively flat land. From the base of the west slope of the Kittatinny Range, it appears as if the mountain extends straight up.

It doesn't There are a succession of steep to very steep slopes interspersed with level lands which vary in width. This particular flat where the deer had travelled and where I was walking was not more than 100 yards wide.

I walked for perhaps ten minutes and then I came upon Jack Bystrak in his tree stand. Good old Jack, at that time in his early 40s and full of vigor. His tree stand was a canvas covered platform heated satisfactorily by a charcoal burning half-gallon bucket stove that he had made himself. The stand had a peaked canvas roof to protect against snow and rain. The stand was some 20 feet above the ground and reached by rungs nailed to two of the cluster of three trees that supported the platform.

It was a well made stand and the closest to the cabin.

The deer had passed within shooting distance of Jack but he had seen them approaching from a long way off, had determined that not one was a buck, and had not fired. I told him that I had tried to kill a doe.

Then I turned, intending to return to my stand but I didn't make it that day. I remember telling Jack that I probably wouldn't see another deer all day and he said, "well, it's early yet. It is only nine o'clock."

So I started walking back north, stepping into my own footsteps, and not making a sound. If it hadn't been for Jack I probably would not have seen the deer because they came from behind me and were soundless because of the powdery snow.

I had gone about 150 yards when I heard Jack shoot both barrels of his old gun, and I whirled in astonishment. Coming right at me, in full flight, was another bunch of about a dozen deer and running directly in the middle of the bunch was a giant of a buck.

He was much larger than any of the other deer and his high spreading antlers made him appear twice as high as the others. My notes of Dec. 10,

This startled buck didn't stare at the camera long before bounding away.

A large doe on a Morris County estate resumed feeding after posing for the camera.

1962, state that the buck passed me at range of 40 yards when I fired at him twice aiming over the back of a running doe.

The buck whirled out of line to cross within 20 feet of me when I fired at him again, and he went crashing down.

The buck whirled out of line to run almost directly at me, crossing at range of 20 feet when I fired the third shell. He collapsed in mid bound and slid forward his head almost buried by the snow.

Any one of those three shells would have been enough to kill him. Barely out of my sight, I heard Jack call from his stand, "Hank, did you get the big buck?" Indeed I had. Poor Jack, he had seen the herd, already running, come angling down the mountain, but the buck was too far to reach. Jack said he fired anyhow to attract my attention.

So I never got back to my stand that day.

There are a few other memories of that great day. When I was dragging the buck down to the camp I saw another deer coming. It stopped within easy range. It was a buck with a pretty fair head but I did not shoot.

I went back to my home in Livingston that afternoon and had the buck on the roof of my then new Volkswagen. I drove down to the Coppermine Inn with the buck and astonished all of the hunters there gathered.

They wanted to know where I got the buck and I told them I had bought it from an old Indian living in a shack on the mountain. I told him that the Indian had three bucks hanging. All were for sale at $1 a point. The 10 pointer cost me $10. I told them that there was a six pointer left for six dollars and a spike buck for two dollars.

How gullible some people are. After I had driven away, one of the hunters asked one of the local authorities how to get to the Indian and his shack. He wanted to buy one of the other bucks.

QUEBEC BROOK TROUT—Fred Roberson, Indian guide at Little Nipissi Lake, with the first four brook trout taken by Henry Schaefer. There are hundreds of three to five pound brook trout in the stream all anxious and willing to take almost any fly or lure. Little Nipissi is about 150 miles north of Lake St. John, Quebec.

# The Camping Trip

My moose hunting safari to Little Lake Nipissi, about 132 miles north of Lake St. John, Quebec, had degenerated into a brook trout fishing expedition, if degenerated is the right word for a spawning run of giants averaging 3-4 pounds. I caught fish as large as five pounds and didn't see any larger although outfitter David Philippe had a picture of his lovely young daughter Alice with an eight pounder.

Petit Nipissi had only one predator in 1949, the brook trout, but Grand Nipissi to the north contained "the renouned Maskinonge reaching the weight 25 & 30 pounds, also lake trout often over the weight of 30 pounds," as was related in Philippe's illustrated Fish & Game Club folder.

On the map the two lakes, connected by a waterfall and rapids, each appear to be nine miles long and three miles wide. They were leased to Philippe by the Province of Quebec as a fishing and hunting preserve. Judging by the signs there were plenty of moose, but in two weeks of hunting with Fred Roberson, my guide, I hadn't seen any.

Fred was employed by Philippe and both lived on the Indian reservation on Pointe Bleue, west of Roberval on Lake St. John. To make this trip I had driven alone from Livingston, N.J., through Quebec City, thence north to Chicoutimi and thence west to Pointe Bleue.

**The only sign of civilization on Little Lake Nipissi in Quebec was this two-tent hunting and fishing camp on a sandy beach at the mouth of a main inlet stream.**

From St. Felicien on Lake St. John, Philippe and I had flown to Little Nipissi with pilot Pat Cormier of Boreal Airways. This was on a Norseman single engine seaplane, and time of flight was one hour. We flew over densely forested liand dotted with many small lakes and streams until we reached our destination.

Camp was a three-army-tent affair on a sandy beach near the southern end of the lake, and not far from a good sized feeder brook. Waiting for us at the lake was Roberson, a taciturn man in his forties who spoke just enough English to get by.

While we were having lunch Roberson caught several big trout from the beach, using a handline with a piece of moose meat on the hook. After lunch the pilot and Philippe took off with the trout, leaving Roberson and myself to spend the next two weeks hunting moose, mostly by paddling along the lake and up the feeder streams.

This was my second moose trip to Quebec and again I failed to see one.

When the plane returned with Felippe he had 19-year old Alice along for a day or two of fishing, but the outfitter was very unhappy about my inability to kill a moose.

Throughout the morning he kept staring at a flaming red and yellow mountain covered with hardwood leaves in their autumnal glory. Spruce and fir surrounded the lake but on this mountain, possibly eight miles away, there was a hardwood forest and Philippe guessed that we should be able to find a moose there.

And so he suggested The Camping Trip.

"We will travel light but carry provisions, spend the night on the mountain, and return tomorrow morning," said Philippe. Roberson said nothing, and I said that it would be an interesting experience.

Roberson carried a small sack with a kettle and the "provisions" inside, tea, a piece of cheese and a half loaf of bread. Philippe carried an ax and I my Model 54 Winchester .30/06 bolt action rifle. This was equipped with the old dependable Lyman Model 48 peep sight.

We traveled to the southern end of the lake by canoe, and then as far up a feeder stream that my two companions could paddle. Then we started tramping toward that magic mountain where I would kill my first bull moose, perhaps.

The display of autumn leaves was beautiful at close range too, but if there was a moose there we didn't see him. Late afternoon turned to dusk and moments before total darkness Philippe announced that it was time to make camp. Using that ax he proceeded to cut eight to 10-inch diameter trees into six foot lengths which he piled on the ground, working almost as fast as a man with a chain saw.

Roberson hung the kettle on a stick above a little fire, using water from a small trickle, and then proceeded to make a bed of spruce boughs which

**David and Alice Philippe and a bush pilot with three of many brook trout caught in Little Lake Nipissi.**

**Alice Philippe of Pointe Bleu, Quebec, with a five-pound brook trout she caught.**

**David Philippe back paddles as his daughter Alice fights a brook trout in a spawning stream of Little Lake Nipissi, Quebec.**

he broke from the trees with his hands.

Our bumpy bough bed was only about three feet high, but the flames from those logs roared 40 feet into the sky. I was sure the two people back at the lake marveled at the sight.

Roberson distributed the evening meal, a piece of cheese and a slice of bread plus a blazing hot tin cup of tea for each man. After dinner both of my friends took off their boots and Roberson put his feet into the provision sack before stretching out.

Perhaps he wanted to keep the bread and cheese warm since his feet were pointed at the fire. Philippe also lay feet to blaze and both were snoring within seconds.

I've never tried sleeping on a bed of nails, but to me those spruce boughs were torture. If I tried sleeping feet to the flames my socks would smoke, while my head froze, and it felt even worse the other way.

After what seemed like hours I dozed off and then I had a nightmare, I thought. I imagined that I was dreaming of a waterfall when actually I was awake, lying on open ground in a rainstorm.

I sat upright to plan a course of action, while Roberson and Philippe slumbered on. The best idea I could come up with was to nudge Phillipe.

"It is raining," he announced. "I fix."

He left to return within minutes with a square piece of birch bark which he handed to me. And I spent the rest of the storm sitting and holding a square of bark over my head while Philippe went back to sleep.

Roberson, still with feet in the bag, slept on blissfully.

In the morning the two awoke. Roberson got his feet out of the sack and divided the rest of the provisions, a piece of cheese and a slice of bread for each man, plus scalding tea of course.

And then we started to hike back to the canoe. The sun came up and with the exertion of walking our clothes started to steam and dry.

And that is how the camping trip ended.

# The Honeymooners

The pool at Oquossoc always held one keeper salmon which lay just behind a big boulder the top of which was barely visible from the point of land below the Rangeley Lake, Maine, dam. The short stream between the outlet which rushes toward Mooselookmeguntic always contained some brook trout of varying size, and immature bright-red spotted land-locks which looked much like brown trout, but with deeply forked tails.

It was pretty much of a waste of time to fish the stream, unless you enjoyed catching and releasing immature salmon. Occasionally a pound to pound-and-a-half squaretail would take your fly, but mostly it was illegal salmon.

Right in the middle of the village and not far from the town of Rangeley, the stream was heavily fished from ice-out into the summer, but if I got there within an hour or so of sunrise there would be nobody else on the scene and I could catch my daily salmon almost every morning. Sometimes it took two or three days for a new fish to move into the spot, and sometimes I took three in three mornings.

Never two fish in a morning. If nothing seized my fly in a half dozen casts I would drive back to the cottage on Greenvale Cove, have breakfast and be in plenty of time for a day on the lake. The lake salmon never seemed to strike during the first few hours of daylight. The story was different after the wind started rippling the water,and the rougher it got the better.

And then one morning when I drove to the pool the honeymooners were there. They were in their low 20s and the bride was sitting on a rock, holding her husband's jacket as all new wives do, and gazing adoringly at her man. He was knee deep in the spot I thought I owned, and casting expertly but not at the right target.

I went to the tail of the pool and did some casting too, not expecting to catch anything to speak of. I caught nothing, and neither did the bridegroom.

After a half hour he gave up and went to sit on a rock close to his wife. And then I did something I've regretted ever since, although I should have forgotten it years ago. I asked the man if he cared if I took a cast or two from the vacated spot.

He said he didn't mind in the least.

So I waded out, made two or three false casts to get the proper range, and dropped the size 10 Black Ghost streamer ten feet above the submerged boulder. There was no need to work the fly. In that current the white marabou fibers would be breathing, and I watched the fly pass above the boulder to be followed by a burst of silver in the deep shadow on the other side.

The salmon promptly went crazy as landlocks on the fly invariably do. It leaped several times but didn't try to leave the pool. It tired and I netted it, about a four-pound fish.

The bride looked as if she was about to cry, and the husband didn't look happy either. I thanked him and tried to tell him the secret of that pool, but the words didn't come.

I drove back to Rangeley with my salmon, and I don't know if I wrecked a marriage or not.

**Big Fritz, the German shorthaired pointer, who was a specialist on clapper rail and woodcock hunting, wanted no part of this wild turkey shot by the author on the Big Spring Game Farm in Sussex County, N.J.**

**Henry Schaefer and Mrs. William Frank of Shrewsbury with a striped bass taken on the Frank's boat by trolling off Sandy Hook.**

**Lillian Schaefer with two kingfish caught off West Palm Beach, Florida.**

Donna, the author's first Brittany spaniel, with pheasants and chukars shot over her points at Burjan's game preserve in Hunterdon County.

A salt water fly rod with 150 yards of backing can take bluefish of any size, and small to medium tuna such as this little tunny.

Inquisitive spike buck.

# The Bugler

It was late in the afternoon in the Bob Marshall Wilderness of Montana on that memorable day in early October, 1967. My partner, Murray Jontow of West Orange, N.J., guide Herbert Hansen and I knew that it would be dark by the time we got back to camp but the weather was beautiful and we didn't have a worry in the world.

Our horses were tied at the edge of a little park on the side of a mountain. We were now only 500 yards or so from them. We were walking along an old and well worn game trail a couple of feet wide. In the morning, riding up this trail, we had seen the tracks of a big grizzly, also abundant droppings indicating that the bear often used this path.

Sign of the grizzly didn't excite us too much because none of us held out any hope of seeing it. The modern day grizzly, in the United States portion of the Rocky Mountains at least, has become as nocturnal as the black bear. He learned a long time ago that his great strength, teeth and claws, are no match for a rifle, and so he remains in heavy timber by day and is almost never seen. In my opinion he remains considerably more numerous than is generally believed.

As we walked down the dusty trail I kept looking for fresh tracks of the bear, but didn't expect to find any and wasn't disappointed. There were none.

To the right of the trail, westerly, the mountain dropped precipitously into a narrow valley and the inevitable stream. Beyond, the real estate angled up sharply again to form another mountain. Directly opposite us, this mountain was heavily timbered in pine. It was in fact a dense forest with no parkland breaks visible.

Herbie, who had been tootling on his obviously brand new elk call from time to time all day, decided to have just one more go at it. Results during the day had been considerably short of sensational. No elk had answered him and none had come a-running, or even walking.

Much has been written about the bugling of the noble wapiti, the king of all the deer. In popular imagination it sounds like a brass bugle, and has been so described by writers who have never heard an elk. Actually, a bull elk's bugling sounds like a kid blowing a tin whistle with a high pitched rise and fall. In the still air of the mountains, at dawn or dusk, you can actually hear it for a mile or more.

Herbie was very fond of his bugle. Hand made, as most of them are, this one was a plastic tube with a plunger inserted at the far end to provide the rise and fall in pitch.

The three of us stopped and Herbie tootled on his plastic whistle. The thin pitched sound rose high, fell away to low, and silence.

Almost immediately, on the mountain directly opposite, about a mile away, somebody or something blew a kid's tin whistle. Startled, the three of us looked at one another in disbelief. A short while later, Herbie, his hands trembling, blew his call once more. Again there was an immediate response, only this time the answering challenge came from farther down on the mountain.

Nobody had to tell anybody else that the elk was coming for us.

As he came closer it became increasingly evident that he was fighting mad. I have never heard wilder noises from anything. He bugled almost incessantly. He bellowed. He barked loudly and rapidly, exactly like an excited dog. I couldn't help thinking that a crazy kid blowing a tin whistle was marching down that mountain accompanied by his yappy dog.

The bull was now climbing our slope and still carrying on. Murray and I had separated to give either of us a better chance, should the elk keep on coming. Murray stayed with Herbie and I was hidden in a clump of dwarf pines at the upper end of a little park. I worried that if the elk did come my way he might be spooked by the horses. I could see one of them 300 yards to my left.

Murray was waiting in the woods 300 yards to my right and Herbie was behind Murray, farther up the slope. He had stopped blowing his whistle, and the elk had become silent also. I could picture the cautious animal circling as he drew closer, getting our wind, and then drifting away in unseen silence.

They do that, you know.

I had just about made up my mind that we had failed when I caught a flash of light and movement down the slope and to my right. The late afternoon sun, now almost down, had flashed on approaching antlers.

There was now no doubt about it, a heavy set of antlers, tossing like a ship in heavy seas, was coming, the body hidden by low pine trees.

Moments later I saw the entire beast. In that waning light the bull looked black. He was walking rapidly and purposefully, climbing steadily and headed directly to the spot where Herbie had challenged him.

That animal's sense of direction was astounding. He had walked about a mile down one steep slope and another mile up to reach us.

At 200 yards the bull passed through a clearing and I fired, missing him completely. He wheeled instantly and started running back through the trees, but the second bullet caught him in the shoulder and the third broke his neck. He collapsed to roll end over end down the steep slope.

He stopped within a dozen feet of the trail the bear had been using. As bulls go he was no record breaker either for size of body or antlers. However, the antlers were heavy, good looking and symetical, with five points to each side.

All we could do that night was dress him out and get the carcass off the ground to cool. I covered the carcass with pine boughs to hide it from scavenging birds, but it was the bear I was worried about. With all the signs on the trail I was sure that the bear used it every night.

I didn't sleep well that night, but the bear didn't find the elk. A wolverine did.

When we rode out with two pack horses the following morning we found that a wolverine had eaten some of the brisket and for some strange reason had wrapped the elk's intestines around its neck, like a macabre necklace.

Fortunately, the wolverine did not befoul the meat  as they are said to do. It was my only experience with a wolverine, and all this one did was eat a little meat and make a necklace.

We quartered the elk and loaded them on the horses along with the antlers. In addition to the wolverine tracks there were fresh grizzly tracks within 20 feet of the elk carcass.

I'll never know why the bear didn't touch the elk.

During the rest of the trip we neither saw nor heard another elk, but Murray shot a mule deer buck. He shot it with my rifle, a Winchester Model 70 .30/06, after his rifle lost its telescope as he was pulling it out of the scabbard on the horse.

That curious buck just stood there looking at us while all this was going on.

**THE TEN POUNDER**—Lillian Schaefer with the "doormat" she caught on the family boat Out in the Open. The fish was taken on a strip of bergall off the "Red Church," St. Michael's, off Takanassee.

# The Ten Pounder

The first Out in the Open was a 15-foot lapstrake skiff powered by a 35 HP Evinrude motor. Aboard this little boat Lillian and I, plus children Betty and Lillian, often fished for summer flounders (fluke) on the rocky grounds off the North Jersey Shore from the upper end of Asbury Park to the Shrewsbury Rocks off Monmouth Beach.

We had what was then our summer home in Shark River Hills and most of the time we fished in the Manasquan River when the boat was docked at Dunwoody's marina at the Route 70 bridge, and then in Shark River after we moved the boat to Main Landing, Belmar.

Both rivers were excellent but each day late in the summer the Belmar party boats that fished for fluke would return from Elberon and Deal with the day's catch of doormats hanging in the stern. They were big fish, from four pounds to seven with an occasional 10 pounder or larger.

In those days, as now, it seems that every other angler you talk to has caught a 10-pound fluke, but fish as big as that are rare. However, few people actually weigh their fish, and most of the ten pounders you hear about were probably much lighter.

The pool winning fish on the party boats are decided on a balance and the weight of the biggest fish is estimated. It is a fair method and it saves buying a new scale every month or so to replace one rusted beyond hope.

The run of the mill fluke are estimated too, and the "two to four-pound fish" you read about were probably only about half that size.

Most of the fluke that move within a mile of the beach and into the estuaries of the Jersey shore each year weigh less than a pound, and have been illegal in that state since 1952 when a law was passed forbidding the sale of fish of less than 14 inches.

The law was sought by commercial fishermen for business reasons, and nobody was worrying about fluke conservation at that time. The fillets you get from a 12-inch fluke aren't much thicker than the skin and weigh about the same. Thin and short fillets don't sell well.

I learned these facts of life when the Out in the Open on its two to four day trips every week started producing a lot more fish than we could possibly eat or give away. To keep on fishing we had the option of releasing the fish, or selling all over 14 inches in length and we chose the latter.

The daily trips were actually 8 to 11 a.m. and each morning I would drive to the market to unload 10-20 pounds of fish. The fish paid the fuel bills and the dock rental, which didn't amount to much in those days.

A 14-inch fluke weighs about a pound and a quarter depending on how much flesh it has on its frame, and fish of that size are much more plentiful than two pounders.

In the early years we never counted individual fish but kept a record of the jumbos only. First we didn't consider a fish of under five pounds a "doormat" but changed that to four pounds when fluke were scarce for a number of years.

Each year we would fasten a Newark News fishing chart and tide table on the wall of the stairs and enter the big fluke. On the good seasons as many as 15 to 20 doormats would be noted on the chart, but never a 10 pounder.

The year 1966 was a good one for big fluke and it started on May 30 when I caught a 4-pound 10-ounce fish and Lillian countered with a 7-pound 9-ounce fish on June 3. I caught an 8-13 fluke on June 17 and a day later Lillian scored with an 8-8 fish right off the bathing beach at McClearie Park, Belmar.

Nearly all of our big fish were caught in Shark River and 11 were noted on the chart that season. The preceeding season there were 15 fish entered and the largest was exactly seven pounds.

During that 1965 season we experienced one fantastic day in the deep channel in front of party boat row when the two of us caught fish of 5½, 6¾ and 7 pounds, in addition to 20 pounds of smaller fish. They were all taken by drifting with cut bait, probably mackerel belly.

This was during an outgoing tide with each drift starting behind Shark River Island and ending close to what was then Dodd's Basin where the three Optimist boats were tied.

I got the five pounder and after Lillian got the 6¾ pounder we went into the tackle shop in the marina to weigh the fish. I suggested we make one more drift and caught the 7 pounder.

Mrs. and Mrs. Jack Bystrak of Chatham were also out on the river that day, and also had one very large fluke in a big catch.

Emil Du Pont of Toms River, who for years paid for his Belmar party boat trips by winning the pools, believed very strongly in big baits for jumbo fluke. He was the first to tie a short shank No. 1 Sproat hook the eye of a long shank Carlisle and fish with seven-inch strips of white and dark side fillets of fluke.

He was convinced that fluke are repelled by human scent so he avoided handling the bait as much as possible. He would fasten the head of a good size fluke to a clip board, and remove the fillets with a knife and fork. As soon as the bait became fouled he would replace it.

My hands never smelled like anything human but more like sea robin, mackerel, bergall, dogfish, squid, killifish, spearing or whatever else we might be using.

Daughter Elizabeth was the first one to catch a seven pounder on the boat, and uncle Dan Schmidt almost got a fish that I am sure was 12 pounds. He hooked it off Deal and thought that he had snagged another rock, until the monster gave two big yanks.

Dan reeled it right to the surface but he was using a very long rod and it was too far out for Lillian to reach even with our huge net. The rim of that net measures 32x28 inches and the handle is 4½ feet, but Lillian couldn't get it to the fish.

The fluke started to thrash, yanked the hook out of its mouth and sank from sight.

Several boats later none of us had yet caught a 10 pounder but I came close with a monster that was an ounce and a half short of nine pounds on the scale at Shark River Marina.

When it finally happened there really wasn't much to it. Lillian and I were drifting off St. Michael's Church off Takanassee Lake at the southern end of Long Branch. This red brick church is a landmark behind the Takanassee Beach Club.

It was a beautiful day in July with a good breeze for drifting but I can't remember how many, if any, fluke we had. Lillian was using a piece of bergall trimmed to shape with a knife and shears, but she recalls that this one was "a junky bait."

Her rod was the same soft-action five footer that was made by Charles Fossani Jr. when he was still a youth selling worms and making rods in Capt. Charlie's bait and tackle shop in Port Monmouth. The reel was a Penn 120 with 20-pound test line.

Even though the bait wasn't pristine a fish grabbed it and Lillian set the hook into something heavy. It felt like a fluke but there were no throbs, no shaking, and no dives for the bottom. It permitted itself to be cranked up without a struggle.

I was standing at the rail with the end of the long net deep in the water, anticipating a power dive as soon as the fish realized it was at the surface. As soon as the fish was above it I moved the bag of the net below it and lifted it into the boat.

It was a perfect specimen, and was in the net before it realized it was in trouble.

Big nets such as the one shown used to be standard on the party boats but come in mighty handy for the six pounds and over fluke that are still being caught. The one shown weighed about three pounds.

# Betty's Fluke

Our first ocean going boat was a 15-foot Estlander lapstrake seaskiff powered by a 25 h.p. Evinrude motor, which we eventually docked at Shark River Hills Marina in Neptune after a season in Brielle and a couple at Belmar Marine Basin, all New Jersey.

The made-in-Denmark boat had classic lines, performed well in the ocean, and was ideal for river fluke fishing since I could troll it in reverse at idling speed. It would travel too fast in forward but just crawled the baits along the bottom in reverse and was the only boat we ever had that could troll a straight course in reverse.

My wife Lillian and daughters Betty and Lillian caught a lot of fish on that old boat, including a few of 4 to 5 pounds, but none of us had ever caught a real "doormat."

On this day we were going to have company, Sunday school superintendent Ed Christiansen of Grace Lutheran Church, Livingston, and his son Carl who went to high school in that town with Betty.

We were going to fish in the ocean on the rocky bottom off Deal, north of Asbury Park, where very large fluke were plentiful in those days. In preparation for the trip I had a supply of fluke "belly" and dark side strips five to seven inches long, at all times considered to be the best baits for doormat fluke off the north Jersey coast.

Emil Du Pont, then living in Newark, was one of about a half dozen expert anglers who paid for their fishing trips aboard the boats out of Belmar Marine Basin with the pool money they won with big fluke. And after pocketing the money Du Pont would sell his fish to a local market.

Du Pont was the inventor of the "killer" hook, a long shank 6/0 turn down eye Limerick with a 1/0 short shank Sproat tied in at the eye of the larger one. Du Pont used a three-foot leader and rather heavy tackle.

He believed that fluke would shy from human scent, so he used a fork to handle his baits, fastening the filet on a clip board and fashioning his baits with a very sharp knife. His baits were six or more inches long, depending upon the size of the fluke he cut up. He never hesitated to use fish longer than the 14-inch marketing size for bait.

Big baits for big fish was his motto and as soon as a bait became sanded he would replace it. Also, he demanded the tip of the bow as his fishing station, so he could always drift his bait away from the boat.

For a few years Du Pont's tackle was always placed in the bow of the party Chief, put there by the mate who knew that he would get a tip from Du Pont upon arrival.

However, Du Pont won so many pools on the Chief the other experts would refuse to sail with him on the boat and Capt. Ralph Mertineit at last was forced to ask him to go with other captains. Equally good at finding big fluke in those days were the late Capt. Pete Saro Sr. of the Spray; and Capt. Frank Cline of the Rambler.

The other boats carried mostly "tourists" who did not want to lose tackle on the rocky bottom which the big fluke favored. On our own boat we seldom lost tackle, because if a rig got hung up, I simply started the engine and backed away from the snag.

But on a party boat a hang up was bound to lead to a broken line and lost tackle. Time was lost by rigging up again. Du Pont always used a light line between the sinker and the swivel since often the hook was not fastened to a rock. He had everything figured out. His line was 30-pound test, the leader about 25, and the line holding the sinker about 10 pounds.

As Out in the Open editor on the old Newark News I frequently rode on the party boats because there was always news to get and things to learn from the other fishermen.

But there is no substitute to having your own boat when it comes to catching a lot of fluke.

So on this day Ed and Carl Christiansen, 16-year-old Betty and I sailed from Shark River Hills Marina, turned north at the inlet and were soon fishing with the big boats off Deal. The Christiansens had bought several big fresh squid and while I told them that fluke was a better bait for fluke, particularly big ones, they persisted in using squid.

So did Betty who cut the squid into long thin strips and loaded both the 6/0 hook and the smaller one with a conglomeration of stuff. The mess looked like nothing living and I told her she was wasting ime.

And indeed, it seemed that she was. To my surprise the Christiansens were catching fluke at a good rate. I was picking up an occasional one on my bait, and Bettty was enjoying the hot sunshine.

And it was hot, about 90, bright sun and dead calm with next to no current to move the boat. We had plenty of bait but were short on drinkables. After a while, Mertineit, whose Chief was close by, called "Hank, do you want some beer and soda?"

I answered that we could love it and as soon as he was ready to make another drift he came moving slowly toward us. His mate was in the bow with cans of liquid in one of those huge, long handled nets the fluke party boats carry. I was standing with my own long handled net and gazing at the faces of the people shoulder to shoulder along both rails, all gazing down at the four people in a little outboard boat on the big Atlantic Ocean.

Just as the mate with the net was directly above us and starting to turn the net with the drinks, Betty had something to say,

"Daddy, I've got a fish on."

She did have a fish on because the rod was throbbing, attached to a fish, and not hung in the rocks.

"Wait a minute," I shouted to Mertineit in the wheelhouse.

Betty had a difficult time getting the fish separated from the bottom, and it pounded heavily as she worked it toward the surface. Suddenly there were shouts, ohs and ahs, and even a few screams from the Chief because the thing that came up was a fluke that seemed to cover a square yard of ocean.

I got it into the net and thence into our huge wicker basket, which just about contained it.

Then we got the soda and beer aboard and as the Chief moved slowly away we heard Mertineit say, "Hank, you'll never get soda and beer from me again."

When I spoke to Ralph by phone that evening he asked me if it weighed 10 pounds. However, while it looked that big from above it was a very thin fish and weighed exactly seven pounds.

It was at that time the largest any of the family had ever caught, our first real doormat.

Dian was little more than a puppy when she posed for this picture with Donna on a day of woodcock hunting.

# Woodcock Hat Trick

Rev. Oscar E. Braune, chaplain of the Newark, N.J. Fire Department and pastor of St. John's Lutheran Church there, was an ardent fisherman as well as a hunter. He always had one or two setters broken on woodcock and quail, although on occasion he would use them for pheasants. The dogs were always excellent, because if they didn't measure up to his standards, Braune promptly got rid of them.

Much of what I learned about woodcock I learned from "Doc" Braune, including the hat trick which he used every time he dropped a bird that the dog didn't retrieve immediately. A bird killed in the air may fall without a trace of scent, and the best of dogs may run right over it without detection. A woodcock has perfect camouflage. The dark and light brown feathers on its back blend so perfectly with the litter on the forest floor it is possible to be staring at a woodcock for minutes without actually seeing it.

Since every spot in the woodcock covers looks just about like every other spot, Braune got into the habit of dropping his big western type broad brimmed fedora at the exact spot where the bird fell. He always took pains to mark the fall, walk to the spot and fix the location with his hat. Then he would thoroughly search around it.

One day, hunting with two friends, Braune killed a woodcock and as usual, marked the fall with the hat. The dog couldn't find it and neither could the dogs of his companions, whom Braune had called in to help.

Braune couldn't find the bird either, and neither did the other two men. They tried to convince him that he had missed, and that they were looking for something that wasn't there. Braune was adamant and searched the spot for another half hour.

Finally, he decided that he had to give up. So he picked up his hat and where do you think the bird was? From then on he always picked up his hat first, but he never again found a bird under it.

Braune started his woodcock hunting career when there were still woods and fields in Irvington and many areas in Union County, but his favorite converts were in the Newark Watershed. Before development, the coverts along the Passaic River in Essex, Morris and Passaic counties provided the best woodcock hunting in North Jersey, although when I lived and hunted in Livingston I did not know it.

The Delaware River flyway always got most of the newspaper publicity, although the hunting always seemed to be much better close to home. Unlike along the Delaware River where shooting was dependent on flight birds, woodcock hunting along the Passaic was excellent from the opening of the season on October 15 of each year.

The coverts in western Essex and eastern Morris County always produced good to excellent crops of birds from parents who never migrated north of the banks of the Passaic and Rockaway rivers.

So dependable was the shooting Joseph Zahn Sr. of Livingston and I once persuaded Newark News photographer Harry Dorer to meet us at the sand pit on Riker Hill at 9 a.m. Harry was waiting for us when we walked out of the woods with our two dogs, an excellent English setter and my Clementine, my first German shorthaired pointer.

Our picture with the eight woodcock limit appeared in the paper, but that was a long time ago when hunting was still a popular sport in rural Essex County and dead game pictures frequently made the papers.

When I started hunting with Braune I considered myself to be a fine shot and owned a 16 gauge Ithaca double barreled shotgun bored modified and full choke, a "hard shooting" gun capable of killing birds at long range. The gun in fact was a good one and took its share of mallards, black and other ducks along the river and the marshes in eastern Morris County.

But the story was different on woodcock.

When Braune's dog or dogs went to point, I always got off the first shot, but most of the time the bird didn't fall until Braune touched off his 12 gauge double gun. When I asked him for an explanation he said his gun was cylinder bored in both barrels.

Compared to my 12-inch patterns at 20 yards, Braune's barrels were printing 30-inch patterns and nearly all of the birds were falling. Also, he bought his shells by the case and practiced at skeet shooting during the off season.

Joe Limon, the Bayonne gunsmith bored all of the choke out of my right barrel and most of the choke out of my left and my field shooting improved dramatically.

Whether hunting with a close working flushing dog or a pointing breed a reasonably fast gun handler is handicapped by a choked barrel, even by so-called improved cylinder, which more properly should be called quarter choke.

Quarter choke works well on pheasants although I prefer skeet or cylinder boring over pointing or close working springers. It is too tight for wookcock and quail despite what you read in the gun catalogs.

The fine old Ithaca 16 was replaced by a 12 gauge Model 21 Winchester Skeet Gun with 26 inch barrels bored Skeet 1 and 2. As far as clay pigeons were concerned it was a bust because of too much muzzle blast, but it was excellent for woodcock, grouse, pheasant, quail, rabbit and squirrel.

With that gun on the old Clinton Public Hunting grounds bagging two cock pheasants on opening day never took more than 30 minutes. After that I would take my springer spaniel Mitzi out into the middle of any big field and give her the command to sit. With all those hunters combing the fields it never took long for the first rabbit to come running by, to be followed by five more.

The limit was six rabbits and two cock pheasants and I always got them, but cottontails and pheasants were very plentiful throughout New Jersey in those days.

Lillian and Betty Schaefer with two landlocked salmon and a trout they helped catch for dinner.

# Chum For Me Pete

The 18-inch rainbow trout I had stocked under the Marksboro bridge of the Paulinskill in mid April, 1954, had not been reported caught, and now it was the first of May. Tags from eight of the 10 fish had been returned to me at the Newark Evening News office and $20 checks were mailed to the lucky anglers.

This was the second year of a study agreed to by the editor of the New Jersey paper. What we were attempting to learn was the relative life expectancy of stocked brook, brown and rainbow trout, their movements in the streams, and what lures or baits were used to catch them.

The Charles O. Hayford State Fish Hatchery at Hackettstown at that time was leaning heavily toward brook trout production. More than half of the 500,000 trout released annually were brook trout and the rest were equal numbers of rainbows and browns.

Hayford, the Oquossoc, Maine native who started the state's first fish hatchery in 1912, was a good friend of mine. What we disagreed on was the brook trout. I argued that the brook trout was much too easy to catch. I wanted more browns for fishing over a longer period of time.

But Charley argued that brook trout were most highly esteemed by the people who bought the licenses, and "the customer is always right." Before coming to New Jersey, Hayford worked at the Ocquossoc hatchery where he reared landlocked salmon and trout, and the trout he worked with in New Jersey came from his beloved Rangeley Lakes.

Alexander "Axle" Gromack of Newark and I fished with Hayford on

Mooselookmeguntic Lake, and I can still see Hayford's face as he told the story of the Indian whose gun had misfired. Hayford's old home was on the short stream which connects Rangeley with Mooselookmeguntic, the lake named after an Indian with a faulty gun.

Hayford's early attempts to raise brook trout to catchable size came off poorly in New Jersey. Unlike in Maine the fingerling trout released in the streams never seemed to grow up, but simply disappeared. Hayford had good success raising rainbows to six or more inches, but the brookies lacked size, color and vigor. But he kept working and eventually developed a strain of brook trout that rivalled the beautiful Maine fish in all respects.

But they sure were easy to catch.

To show the "old" man up I had first bought 10 big brook trout from the Greenwalk Trout Hatchery, Bangor, Pennsylvania, in April, 1953. They were distributed in Big Flat Brook, Paulinskill, Pequest, Musconetcong and South Branch of the Raritan rivers, the "Big Five" in New Jersey.

They were released on the 17th of the month and three were caught the first day. Four were caught on April 18, and the other three were caught on April 19, 22 and May 10.

The thing that surprised me the most about this experiment was that one brook trout had managed to live for 23 days in a heavily fished stream. It was caught on a worm with spinning gear, which was then just coming into use. Seven of the other fish were caught on flyrods and mostly on worms.

The ability of a small percentage of hatchery brook trout to survive heavy angling pressure was later to be proved by electro-shocking of the streams. The state biologists who did the shocking always seemed to find one brook trout among many browns and rainbows, and large numbers of warm water fish, including an astonishing number of eels.

The same five streams were used in my 1954 stocking, and as expected the first to die were the four brook trout. One, stocked above the Schaefer Bridge on Big Flat Brook, survived for less than a minute.

People were fishing from the bridge, one man on the upstream side who was dangling a waterlogged piece of worm from the hook of a spinner just inches below the surface. There were cars parked along the road and with the fish in the net I had to walk about 100 feet to get to the bridge and then about 30 feet up stream where I took the gasping trout out of the net and tossed it into the stream.

Then I walked back and just as I reached the road people started yelling, because the man with the waterlogged bait had hooked the trout. It was about two pounds and 17 inches, but the man just hauled it toward shore and out of the water.

I retrieved the tag and paid the angler his $20 prize money.

The other three brookies lasted a few days. The rainbow returns came in quite fast too to be followed by two of the three browns. And on the first day of May only an 18-inch brown stocked below Layton on the Big Flat and the Paulina rainbow were still at large, or at least unaccounted for.

The brown trout survived for two months before it was caught in the same pool into which it had been released. It was taken on a wet fly during the flies only season. The pool is deep, a big boil below a steep bank right next to the road but is best fished from the east bank. That wary trout had passed up hundreds of worm and salmon egg baits in April not to mention scores of spinners and flies before it finally mistook an artificial fly for a real insect.

The Marksboro stretch of the Paulinskill was a great favorite of the North Jersey Sportsmen's Club, members of which included Joe Zack, Howard Spangenberger, Dick Lasky, Axle Gromack, Arthur Krieger, Charlie Bicker, Chet Natress, Joseph Ciesielski, Eddie Stari, Pete Hubiak, John Whatton and the writer.

We had built a log cabin on Little Swartswood Lake and for years used it for fishing and hunting. The Marksboro stretch was the closest big stream to the cabin, and I had hoped that a fellow member would take the prize trout.

But I did not tell them where I had stocked any of the fish, and I did not fish the Paulinskill pool myself while the rainbow remained unaccounted for.

One day Stari looked down over the bridge on the up stream side to watch Pete fishing salmon eggs with fly tackle directly below. Pete had his back to the wall above the bridge and was letting his line run down into the deep pool under the bridge. On every drift Pete had a take, and every time came up with an empty hook.

"Let me show you how to catch that fish," said Stari, and started to climb down to the water without being invited, but Pete grudgingly moved out of position to let his friend try his hand.

"Lend me a salmon egg," said Stari and after impaling the egg on the hook continued, "Now chum for me Pete." The latter tossed a half dozen eggs into the stream and they and the one with the hook in it disappeared on their way down to the bridge.

You have probably guessed that Start hooked the big rainbow with the tag in it on his very first drift. But you probably haven't guessed that he was in my office the next morning with the tag.

"Pay me the money," said Stari.

For many years the Beaver biplane was the workhorse for air transportation in the Canadian bush. The man on the pontoon is Edgar Baird, outfitter, and the place is Newton Lake, Newfoundland.

Henry Schaefer and daughters Betty and Lillian at a Livingston riding academy.

The moose that wore this unimpressive set of antlers was a herd bull with a harem of a dozen cows plus calves. The author took him because it was his turn to shoot a moose that day, and none of the other half dozen bulls surrounding the herd had much of a head either. The machine is a muskeg tractor.

The screened meat house (right) will be well filled with moose quarters by the time the sleigh at left is unloaded. The two oxen were used to carry the four quarters of each moose from the scene of the kill to the sleigh. The man in the picture is Percy Taylor, one of our two guides.

Seven sets of moose antlers atop of the boat that will carry the men and a few tons of meat from North Bay, to Port Aux Basques, Newfoundland, for the ferry ride back to Nova Scotia and ultimately home.

**Joe Zahn, left, Henry Schaefer and our two dogs with an eight bird limit of woodcock taken on the morning of opening day on Riker Hill, Livingston, New Jersey.**

121

Committee members surround the first dedication of the Kenneth F. Lockwood Memorial in the gorge of the South Branch of the Raritan River in 1950. The first editor of the Out in the Open column in the Newark News died in 1948. The first bronze plaque was stolen but was replaced by Trout Unlimited in 1973.

# El Monstroso

Tarpon to an estimated 150 pounds were "jumped" by the four fishermen in the party of eight newspaper, magazine and promotions persons during a visit to Guatemala under a still stable government in September, 1979.

The monstrous tarpon, by far the largest I have ever seen over a span of more than 20 years in trips to tropic and semi-tropic lands, was hooked in Lake Petuxbatun by Jerry Kenney, outdoors editor of the Daily News, New York, who was fishing with me and our guide Eufracio Bolon, in a 30-foot dugout powered by a 9½-horsepower Mercury engine.

Jerry, after losing both of his total stock of two plugs, was fishing with a Creek Chub Pikie Minnow, a fresh water plug that ha been in my tackle box for 30 years. On the previous day I had failed to get a single strike on that plug, but "El Monstroso" grabbed it on Jerry's fifth or sixth cast.

The fish struck 10 feet from the boat, thrashing an eight-foot circle into froth before making a 15-foot high leap to pop the 15-pound test spinning line.

The Indian guide, who looked in his 50s, and who had turned several shades to the white, and was trembling, shouted "El Monstroso" before calming down. Asked how long he thought the fish was, he extended one arm to the sky indicating a total length of seven to eight feet.

The hugh fish was the highlight of three days of fantastic tarpon fishing on this large and very deep lake deep in the jungles of northwestern Guatemala. According to Ana Smith, managing director of the Panamundo Guatemala Travel Service, our tour director, it had never been fished before by nonresidents.

We lost track of the number of fish hooked and jumped, tarpon that ranged from a minimum of 15 pounds to 75 or 80. We lost a lot of fish but would have released most of them anyhow. We brought just three 15 to 25 pounders back to our camp. They were smoked in a 55-gallon steel drum by Albert Edward Gillet, the head guide, and for the first time in my life I dined on tarpon.

According to everyone I ever met in Florida, tarpon are inedible.

Smoked tarpon, in my opinion, is not up there with smoked whitefish, salmon, trout, whiting, eel and some of the others, but everybody else who ate it said it was delicious.

We were the guests of the Guatemala Tourist Commission which was seeking to bring sportsmen and women to sample the fishing and hunting in this unexploited land.

Reportedly the lake also contains large numbers of snook and peacock bass, but we were there toward the end of the rainy season and the lake was very high, and the snook and bass were deep in the trees and under water brush and could not be reached by boat.

According to Gillett, the tarpon are available throughout the year, with fishing best during the rainy season. During the dry season, October through March, smaller tarpon but plenty of snook and bass prevail.

Bob Nesoff of M. Silver Associates, Inc., New York, public relations firm, could obtain just sketchy information on the type of fishing we might find. The problem was the language barrier, translating Spanish fish into English. We were told that we could be fishing for "shad, haddock and white fish."

This left us with absolutely nothing to go on, but Nesoff said that there might be tarpon, so I carried a medium weight spinning and a bait casting outfit with 15 and 12-pound test line. I thought the fish in a lake would be small. The reels were a Daiwa 1600C and an Ambassadeur 6000. The rods were a Garcia Conolon 2510C seven-foot light action and a Fenwick F7357 six-foot bait caster. Into a cardboard box I jammed a half dozen blue and white Rebel plugs, two Pikie Minnows, and a few other plugs, spoons and spinners.

Since the tarpon would have nothing to do with the blue and white Rebels and since these were soon the only plugs we had left, we obtained from Gillett a small can of yellow paint and I made yellow plugs out of the blue and whites.

This was all quite miraculous in a jungle camp, and the tarpon went bananas for yellow plugs. Other minor miracles included the manufacture of three gaffs. One was made by me, a big nail hammered through a mahogany stick, and two were made by the Indians, utilizing a copper rod, slightly sharpened, and attached to a wooden handle.

The copper gaffs were the most fun because they always straightened when trying to lift a fish aboard. There were no steel gaffs in camp. The natives don't use them. I was told they troll spoons on stout handlines or rope and drag the fish aboard.

The fishing reminded me of bass and pickerel on a U.S. lake, but instead of plugging the shortline we plugged the edge of trees jutting above water. I judge the lake level to be 25-30 feet higher than what it would be toward the end of the dry season.

Kenney raised easily 10 fish to my one on the first day, because he was using my spinning outfit and could drop his plug closest to the trees. Also, he had the bow position.

The first man to drop a plug close to trees along an undisturbed stretch of water always had an excellent chance for a strike, if not immediately, after the first few turns of the handle.

The tarpon's reaction was always the same, a crazy gill rattling leap, to be followed by a succession of small runs and further leaps. None tried diving into the submerged treetops.

They just leaped and made short surface runs until they turned over, and then came the comedy act of trying to impale them through the skin of the lower jaw, and watch the copper gaff straighten as we tried to lift the fish into the dugout.

The hollowed out tree was comfortable to fish from after we laid boards across the rails for seats. The guide poled the boat along the shoreline while we fished.

Most of the natives had never seen rods and reels before, and I am sure they thought we were extremely inefficient. It would probably have been much more productive to troll a lure on 100-pound test line with the motor running and haul the fish in over the rail.

Lake Petexbatun is a for real miracle. It drains into the Rio de la Pasion which flows for 20 miles west to the Mexican boarder and its conflux with the Rio Usumacinto. This river flows north along the border and then into Mexico proper, and according to Ramon Starr, camp manager, eventually into the Gulf of Mexico.

Starr says the big tarpon come into the lake to spawn, making a journey of hundred of miles to do so.

Others in the party included Mike De Pasquale of River Vale, Curtis Winston of Flanders, both New Jersey, C. Boyd Pfeiffer of Phoenix, Maryland: Nesoff, and Maggie and Mike Nichols of New York.

Both Pan American and Eastern flew to Guatemala City, the "Hub of Central America," and a real fun city with perfect 68-72 degrees year around temperature. The jungle is hot by day but not any hotter than New Jersey during the summer.

There are insects but nothing to compare to the demons that infest the south Jersey salt marshes. During my stay in the jungle I wore a T shirt, shorts, socks, convas boat shoes and a cap. The insects didn't bother me nor were any of us threatened by venemous reptiles, scorpions, jaguars or orther wild beasts.

Five volcanos are visible from the hotel tops of bustling Guatemala City and one of them, Fuego, was active and belching fire and smoke.

# NOTES

# NOTES